I0609659

Francois Guènon, Thomas J Hand

**Guenon on Milch Cows**

A treatise upon the bovine species in general

Francois Guènon, Thomas J Hand

**Guenon on Milch Cows**
*A treatise upon the bovine species in general*

ISBN/EAN: 9783337183509

Printed in Europe, USA, Canada, Australia, Japan

Cover: Foto ©Andreas Hilbeck / pixelio.de

More available books at **www.hansebooks.com**

# GUENON

ON

# MILCH COWS.

A TREATISE UPON

## THE BOVINE SPECIES IN GENERAL.

TRANSLATED FROM THE LAST AND ENLARGED EDITION OF F. GUENON.

BY

## THOS. J. HAND.

ILLUSTRATED.

NEW YORK:

ORANGE JUDD COMPANY,

751 BROADWAY.

1883.

# TRANSLATOR'S PREFACE.

The Version in English of Guenon's Treatise through which his system became known to American Breeders, Dairymen, and others, was Mr. Trist's translation, made more than thirty years ago, from the first French edition, published long before the Author had completed his observations and studies.

To its incompleteness and consequent defects may be attributed much of the lack of appreciation with which the system has met. For its fair and intelligent discussion an accurate knowledge of its Author's mature conclusions is requisite. This the Translator offers as his contribution.

As there are no infallible external signs of milk-giving capacity, exceptions will be met with; but as Mr. Mackie has observed: "A cow having originally a natural capacity for copious milk-giving may by some cause, perhaps altogether unknown, be converted at an early age into a very moderate milker, and yet retain all the external signs of good dairy quality. The head may remain small, her throat clean, her neck thin, her body wedge-shaped, her tail long and slender, etc., etc., and yet the yield of her udder be greatly reduced by some of the causes above alluded to, whether known or unknown. These external dairy-marks are not discredited on account of numerous exceptions to their reliability, and the same is true of the escutcheon. As a general rule, cows having good escutcheons are good cows; and the reverse. In those parts of Europe where cows have for generations been worked under the yoke, the escutcheon has almost entirely disappeared ; whereas in the dairy races, like the Dutch, the Ayrshire, the Jersey, and the native American, the escutcheon is generally of large size in all good milkers."

If, then, Guenon's system will but enable any one to know at sight a good cow from a bad one, and to select the best animals out of a herd; and especially if it enables one to choose the best calves and young heifers without waiting until they have grown up to maturity, is it not of great value ?

The frequent repetitions to be met with in the text are to be explained on the ground that the book is intended for reference and consultation, and therefore the Author has given the necessary information at every point, without presupposing a perfect memory on the reader's part of all that precedes.

The only portions of the original work that have been omitted are some chapters relating to certain local breeds in France, that do not possess interest or value to American readers.          T. J. H.

*New York.*

# MILCH COWS.

## THE AUTHOR'S ACCOUNT OF HIS DISCOVERY.

Error seems to be propagated with the velocity of light. Every obstacle disappears before it, and everywhere it is welcomed. Truth, on the contrary, is usually received with indifference, and often with doubt, mistrust, or suspicion. How often have we seen the originator of a discovery which, accepted and put in practice, would augment the wealth, and increase the well-being of a community, wrecked upon hatred, ignorance, and envy, and become the scorn of the learned, who regard him as ignorant, and the laughing-stock of fools, who look upon him as a lunatic. Too weak to struggle against such odds, he perishes in the contest, leaving to his opponents the glory of having—perhaps for ages to come—buried his discovery in oblivion, and to the public, the loss of an unknown advantage.

If—happier than these martyrs of new ideas—I had at last succeeded, after twelve years of incessant struggles, in making the truth of my discovery obvious to all, nothing would then remain for me but to express my gratitude to those generous friends who had aided me, and to leave to those who so firmly supported and encouraged my efforts, the care of popularizing and disseminating my method.

During the many years which have passed since I gave to the public the first edition of my "Treatise on

Milch Cows," men of science and practical breeders have given it great attention. When they saw its application by myself, and beheld the accurate estimate which I was able to make, by merely looking on animals, which I then beheld for the first time, they were greatly surprised, so far did the success surpass their expectation. And yet, to my thinking, there is nothing in the fact which science can not explain.

As this work is entirely of a practical character, I have thought it best to leave to anatomists the task of furnishing more complete details of the nature and conditions of the milk-giving organs and function. These researches, however valuable, are not essential to the farmer or breeder. What he needs is to be able to judge an animal by visible external signs. There are, in the vegetable kingdom, positive signs by which we may recognize, even at the time of planting it, the vital force of a tree, the form and savor of the fruit it will bear, the epoch of its maturity, and the use to which it may be put when cut down. These qualities are recognizable by the color of the bark, the tints and specks upon the rind, the buds, the foliage, etc. And so it is in the animal kingdom, but especially in the bovine race.

My first studies were in arboriculture, which I practised with my father for several years, my principal occupations being the trimming of trees, grafting, and budding. In studying vegetables, I caught the idea and an insight into the principle of classification. Thus I was better prepared for my future work in the classification of the bovine race, a work which no one had even attempted, either theoretically or practically. My classification by characteristic signs includes various breeds, without distinction of age or sex. Although these signs have always existed, they have heretofore escaped the observation of all, even of the most distinguished animal-painters, and of the most eminent veterinarians.

My method is destined to create an epoch, for it attacks and overthrows the old prejudices and conventional ideas which have been in force hitherto. It opens a new era to an art in its infancy, and to a science of which even the first principles have been unknown—it is necessary, therefore, that I set it forth with the most elaborate details. The present edition of my work, enriched by a multitude of new observations, differs largely from the first, in which I had limited myself to explaining the characteristic signs of milk-production. In this new work I embrace all which can interest and instruct the buyer or owner of cattle; but the milk-product is still the special object of my attention. We may say that the Milch Cow is the principal source of wealth to the agriculturist. I here give perfect instructions to estimate its worth, to classify it, pronounce upon the value and persistence of its milking, distinguish with exactness the qualities which should combine in a faultless animal, etc.

I have shrunk from no sacrifice of time, labor, and care, to complete my work. In a subject so novel, I could have no master but myself, and no book but Nature. As I advanced in knowledge, difficulties without number arose in my path, and it has only been by great toil and close thought that I have succeeded in overcoming them and reducing my ideas to lucid order. It is not a treatise of natural history that I have written, but simply the results of my innumerable observations, and in stating these results, I use the ordinary language of daily life, believing that thus I shall be better understood by those to whom I address myself, and who, like myself, are unfamiliar with the technicalities of science.

Compelled to create an entirely new nomenclature, and to give new names to objects heretofore unknown or completely neglected, I reasoned thus :

If my mode of expression is clear and precise enough

for persons of little information, I can not doubt that it will be so for those who are better instructed, and in placing my method thus within the reach of all grades of intelligence, I shall have accomplished the object which I had in view. This method of mine is of extreme simplicity, and whoever shall know thoroughly the escutcheons of the first order of each class, will be able to form a judgment of all.

The escutcheons are ten in number: they extend, according to the class, from the center of the four teats to the level of the upper extremity of the vulva,* and in width may reach from the middle of the hinder surface of one thigh to that of the other. According to their form and configuration, the escutcheons distinguish the ten families which together compose my classification—this is the simple expression of a system which has been represented as so complicated.

A special figure appended to each class, serves to designate the "bastards." Each of the classes or families is characterized by an escutcheon of definite form, always preserving that form, but variable in its superficial dimensions. This surface might be measured by square centimetres,† but that would be too complicated for practical use, as it is modified by the general size of the animal. In my system it is measured by its natural boundaries, which are the houghs, the inner surface of the thighs, and the vulva. This surface of the escutcheon, of variable extent, allows me to divide each class or family into six orders, to each of which I assign—taking also the size of the animal into consideration—the quantity, quality, and persistence of its milk, as indicated by

---

* The portion of the female generative organs visible externally.

† The hundredth part of a metre, the French standard measure of length. It is about two-fifths of an inch, or accurately .39371 of an inch. In the translation its equivalent is given in inches and decimal parts of an inch.

the characteristic features.  The escutcheon of the first order is most amply developed, and its indications are therefore the best.  That of each of the five following orders resembles in pattern the first, but on a reduced scale.  I have added to this new edition :—

1. Two new classes, subdivided also into six orders.

2. Two varieties of escutcheons having certain points of similarity with the others.

3. The classification of bulls intended for propagation.

These three additions complete and generalize my system.  The new forms of escutcheons were known to me at the time of the publication of my first edition, but they were of such rare occurrence in the breeds which I had then studied, that I thought it unnecessary to introduce them.  Since that time, however, I have discovered in my numerous journeys in France and abroad, that there are breeds in which they occur more frequently, and I have therefore assigned them their proper places in my classification.  As for the two new varieties of escutcheons, they are added as a sort of appendix, and show the results of crossings between two classes.

In the first edition of this work I had divided each class into eight orders.  These I still retain; but, as the seventh and eighth are of rare occurrence, I place them by themselves outside of my regular classification, which I thus simplify.  After fully describing and classifying the "free" cows (those whose milk continues after a new impregnation), I pass to the bastards, or those which, while perfectly resembling the others in form and color, have the essential difference that they lose their milk as soon as they are again with calf.  The signs by which these bastards may be distinguished, I have indicated with the utmost precision.

After the bastards, follows a chapter on bulls.  In this I have reduced the orders to three:—good, medium, and bad—these terms having reference to the ability of the animal to beget a progeny of good milking qualities. The same signs, with certain modifications, which in the cow denote a good milker, in the bull denote the capacity to beget good milkers.

Although the classification has special reference to the milking or reproductive qualities of the animal, yet it is important to take into consideration all those other qualities which it may possess, and should possess, to be of a faultless organization. In all the breeds, cows of the first and second orders of each class, will give a greater quantity of milk than cows of the lower orders, under similar circumstances. To know the absolute milk production of any cow, it is necessary to know what is the usual food of cattle in the region to which it belongs, and this known, by following the indications of the escutcheon, the daily yield of any cow of that locality can be closely estimated.

A cow, to give her maximum of milk, should be neither too fat nor too lean. If the cow be lean and under-fed at the time of calving, her yield of milk will be impaired, and though more generous diet may restore her strength, she will not recover her full flow of milk until a second calving.

A large milker, however disposed to fatten, and however fat she may be at the time of calving, becomes lean fifteen or twenty days after the birth of her calf. The periods of rutting are also further apart with her than with poor milkers, as her vital powers are more enfeebled by the heavy strain upon them.

A milch cow may be compared to a fruit tree, which bears more fruit some years than others. When the sap tends strongly to the production of fruit, the growth of the wood is almost stationary. When, on the contrary, the tree bears but little fruit, the sap tends to the increase of the wood, and then, after a longer or shorter rest, the production of fruit is increased. In the same way it is seldom that a cow keeps the same yield for three consecutive years; her food sometimes tending to increase her bulk and fat, at the expense of the milk, and at other times going almost entirely to the milk production. These variations may depend upon differences of the seasons, and their effect upon the plants and herbage upon which the cows feed.

Cows reared in fine pastures will exceed the product which I have assigned to their class and order, while those in poor or marshy pastures will fall short of it, unless the deficiency be supplied by generous feeding in the stable. The effect of these differences is so great, that cows which, in rich pastures, or abundantly fed, will give from 20 to 25 litres of milk daily, transported to poor pastures will have their yield diminished one-half.

My readers will therefore understand that in the estimates of my classification, I do not pretend to give rigorous and absolute figures, but only an approximate quantity for each class and order, founded on an average of various breeds and localities. I will also mention here, that in the approximate weight which I assign to animals in that part of my work which treats of the fattening of beeves, etc., I follow the usual custom, and refer to the carcass, cleared of head, feet, hide, intestines, etc. In estimating the weight on the hoof, the figures would be greatly increased, sometimes even doubled.

The significance of the escutcheon, or figures formed by a reversal of the direction of the hair, has hitherto escaped all observers, even those most interested in knowing it. Indeed, the effect produced by this change of direction, is not glaringly conspicuous: it is a mere difference of shade or lustre, between the escutcheon, and the hair surrounding it. The hair of the escutcheon is shorter, finer, softer and more silky, and at the first glance appears as if freshly shaven.

All animals of the bovine race, domesticated or wild, are marked with an escutcheon of some form, and this characteristic sign is transmitted from parent to offspring.

I have taken no account of that part of the escutcheon which lies under the belly towards the navel, the part lying on the udder and between the haunches, which is always visible when the animal is standing, being sufficient for all purposes. But to see the escutcheons in all the development which is given them in my figures, the udder of the animal must be thoroughly distended with milk, so that the hind legs are widely separated. In this way the escutcheon is shown as if the skin were stretched out on a flat surface, and all the parts exposed which are hidden in the folds of the udder and thighs.

To get a perfect view of the escutcheon, the observer should stand behind the animal and make it take several steps forward, that the movement may bring all the parts successively into view. We may also, by brushing the hair downwards with the hand, bring out more directly its form and dimensions.

Though my method may seem to be complicated at first, it really is not so, it can be mastered with little trouble. Its whole nomenclature consists of three terms, and its whole mystery in recognizing the forms which these terms designate. These terms are "escutcheons," "ascending feathers," and "descending feathers," and when the student knows thoroughly these signs and their significance, he understands my method as well as I do myself.

The feathers, as will be seen, share with the form of the escutcheon in distinguishing the orders, they multiply the subdivisions, and seem to render my system more complicated; but as they have incontestable and important value, I could not omit them.

If on certain animals, the form and size of the characteristic signs should not seem to correspond exactly with any of my figures, but to be intermediate, as it were, between two classes, the observer should note the class and order to which they approach most nearly, and from that make a probable estimate.

Beauty of form represents to me only an ideality, and though it deserves to be considered, it is only as an accessory, and of no value in estimating the yield of milk. I have, however, not neglected to treat of those features which characterize a regular and beautiful form. I also speak of the mode of recognizing the age of an animal by the teeth and by the horns.

May this work, the fruit of my life's experience, justify the honor which has been done me by the numerous agricultural societies who have conferred membership upon me, and by the government, which has borne part of the expense of this edition, with the two-fold object of encouraging me in my work, and of facilitating the dissemination of my method.

# BOOK I

## CHAPTER I.

### THE BOVINE RACE.

In this race of animals the farmer finds his most valuable resources. In many countries the cow is man's
assistant in the labors of the field; while everywhere,
among rich and poor, milk forms a staple article of food,
and of all domesticated creatures, she is to-day the most
indispensable to the human race. Many naturalists have
left us valuable treatises on this race of animals, and
especially on the milch cow; but all their writings
abound in anatomical and physiological descriptions.
They have, it is true, enriched science with useful information and with original theories, but down to the present time they have not revealed to us the specific characteristics of those cows which are good milkers. They
have confined themselves to sundry vague and often
erroneous indications; my system has never been even
suspected by them, and for this reason my method is as
novel in its principles as in their application.

### THE BOVINE SPECIES IN GENERAL.

Before entering upon particular descriptions, it will be
as well to glance at horned cattle in general, adding cer-

(16)

tain new observations upon the production of milk, which is the main object to which my method is directed. Although scientific writers are unanimous in admitting that the good or evil qualities of each parent affect the offspring, this essential point has been too much neglected in the practice of farmers and breeders, who, for the most part, are not sufficiently enlightened to discern their true interests. While they aim at preserving herds pure, and improving them, they exercise no proper care in pairing the males and females, giving a cow of one class* to a bull of another, from which union results a hybrid offspring, more or less inferior to its parents.

My experiments, prolonged through a period of more than thirty-five years, have proved that from the union of a bull of large size and of the first order, with a cow of less size and lower order, there results an offspring stronger and of higher order than the mother; while if the superiority be in the cow, the calf will be inferior to her in milking qualities. Thus a bull of the first order in any class, joined with a cow of an inferior order, will produce an offspring superior to the mother, and this superiority of the offspring will always occur, in every class, when the parents have been chosen from the first order of that class. If, on the contrary, the parents are chosen from different orders and classes, the resulting progeny most frequently will belong to neither the class of the sire nor that of the dam. In this way arises the phenomenon of bastardy, which rapidly brings about the degeneration of the breed.

### BASTARDS.

Every class has its bastards, that is to say, individuals which, while they resemble the higher orders of their classes, differ from them in milking qualities, and it is

---

* What the author means by the terms class and order, will be explained further on.—Tr.

this resemblance which leads imperfect judges into continual errors.*

## OF THE UTILITY OF THE METHOD, AND THE CHARACTERISTIC SIGNS ON WHICH IT IS FOUNDED.

It is therefore a matter of essential importance that cows shall be served by none but bulls of good quality. But how are these to be distinguished? To this my method gives the answer. The characteristic signs are the same with males as with females. It is true that in the former they are less developed; but by giving the necessary attention and consulting the figures which illustrate my classification, they can easily be recognized. These characteristic signs, in all the classes and all the orders, are external; they are quite independent of the color of the hair or the figure of the animal. These latter features have nothing to do with my classification, and I only use them to a limited extent as indications of the probable origin of a certain type or individual, of the country to which it belongs and the place of its birth.

It is certainly a great point gained to be able to distinguish at sight between a good and a bad cow; to estimate the average yield of animals of different nature under the same system of feeding and care; but my discovery goes farther than this. My method may be applied to the youngest calf, and by the indications of the escutcheon alone the future milking qualities of the animal may be predicted. In fact, these indications are more distinct on the young calf than on the adult cow, the qualities to which they owe their origin being inherent in the constitution of the animal. It comes into the world with the signs of its good or bad nature distinctly marked upon it, easily distinguishable by even an indifferent judge, at the very day of its birth.

* The signs by which bastards may be recognized are given at the end of each class.

At birth the hair of the escutcheon is downy, and at the margins of contact with the surrounding skin, it is long and silky. A few days after birth its figure is not so plain as at the age of six weeks or two months, because at this time the downy or velvety hair falls off, leaving the escutcheon naked. From the period of birth the escutcheon develops and enlarges with the growth of the body; it enables us at all times to form a judgment of the animal, whether male or female, and serves as a certain indication of its future value. Every animal is so marked, and long experience has shown that on the fœtus of seven and a half or eight months—at which time the skin is smooth—it is more conspicuous than in the calf at full term, when the hair is long and silky, and sometimes inclined to bristle.

Breeders may now, by this guide, easily separate good from inferior animals; may distinguish those which are fittest for fattening, and reserve for dairy purposes those cows which will give the largest yield of milk and butter. In the cities, I trust, we shall have no fraudulent adulterations; but the public will be supplied with an abundance of pure milk, and infants will no longer be fed upon a thin or unwholesome liquid which poisons the young life which it is meant to nourish. The more abundant any product is, the better is its quality. If the production of milk be doubled or tripled, that of butter will increase in a like proportion, and economy and public health will both be the gainers.

In what I have stated there is no exaggeration. Simple as my method is, it is really of an importance which it is not easy to over-estimate.

## OF THE COLOR OF CATTLE.

As a general rule, each country has its peculiar color; thus in whole provinces one sees nothing but red cows of various shades; in others, black; in others again, white, black and white, red and white, and so forth. The qualities of the cow, therefore, bear no relation to the color of the hair.

## INFLUENCE OF CLIMATE.

Among the causes which lead to the degeneration of our breeds of cattle, must be reckoned the influences of climate and feeding, for although, as a general thing, the inferior breeds are more widely distributed than the good, there are yet districts where good breeds are predominant, as for instance, Flanders, Normandy, Brittany, Auvergne, and others.

Cows and heifers of good milking-breeds, transported to other countries, preserve their original qualities during life; but if these cows are crossed with the bulls of the country, the offspring is inferior to the mother, either in size or in milking qualities. So the owner who wishes to have none but the best milkers, is obliged to recruit his stock continually from abroad.

## OF THE PURCHASE OF COWS AND HEIFERS.

In France, cows and heifers are constantly transported from one province to another, but bulls rarely, and yet the reproduction of the good qualities of the females, depends entirely on these. From this neglect come unsuitable crosses, which always yield a degenerate offspring.

It must be borne in mind that there are breeds of superior milkers, which, with escutcheons of similar form and extent, give a far larger yield to the pail. But this yield will always bear a relation to the fineness of the hair and the color of the skin, even when the animals are living in a country foreign to that of their origin, as they still preserve their original type, and do not lose their specific qualities. Hence in all places and among all breeds, the first and second orders of each class are those which have the highest value, and which must always be preferred.

## NECESSITY OF AVOIDING INJUDICIOUS CROSSES.

It is not in the power of either the farmer or the stock-raiser to change the climate of his district, but at least he has the means of preventing the deterioration of his breeds, in a judicious system of crossing; and in this, by the use of my method, he is secured from a multitude of errors.

How frequently does it happen, that animals selected for supposed good qualities, and carefully raised, turn out worthless, while those have been sent to the butcher, which would richly have repaid all their owner's care, had he known how to distinguish them. And the inferior cows are too often crossed with still worse bulls, so that the degeneration is accelerated rather than resisted, to the disappointment and heavy loss of the owner.

On what principles of selection have breeders hitherto proceeded? They are guided by form for the most part, and judge of the future offspring by the size, the build, the origin of one or the other parents. Yet experience shows that these signs are often deceptive, and we see cows which present the noblest appearance, large size, and perfect figure, wanting nothing, in fact, except—milk.

## FORM OF BULLS.

Though I have said that the form of the animal has no value in determining the quantity of milk, yet I recognize the fact that those bulls will best fulfill the wishes of the breeder, which are well proportioned, the sides well rounded out, the flanks narrow, the neck massive, the head short and square, the ears hairy inside, which is a mark of strength and spirit; the horns short, and of medium thickness.

## FORM OF COWS.

These should be of good shape and proportion, the head small and square, eyes large and bright, shoulders narrow, back level, rump well formed, haunches wide, thighs round, the udder not too long, round, elastic, and covered with silky down.

I have noticed that in general, those cows which have four equal teats, and those which have six (four equal and two smaller ones which usually yield no milk,) belong especially to the higher orders of their class, and that those of inferior orders, have usually four teats, with one false nipple.

# CHAPTER II.

## THE UDDER AND LACTIFEROUS VESSELS.

SUMMARY.—The uselessness of anatomical knowledge in distinguishing milking qualities.—The udder.—The cutaneous veins.—The milk veins.

## THE USELESSNESS OF ANATOMICAL KNOWLEDGE IN DISTINGUISHING MILKING QUALITIES.

In a practical treatise on cows, having special reference to their milking qualities, the milk-giving organs can be considered only with reference to their external appearance. All other details would be useless to the practical breeder.

In two cows of the same breed, of similar size and equal weight, the mammary glands may exhibit the same bulk, while they are far from possessing the same capacity, the difference being caused by the greater or less diversity of the tissue of which they are composed.

An udder may be large and apparently distended with milk, while in reality its bulk is due to a mass of spongy tissue, and the yield of milk will bear no proportion to the volume of the bag. We must look elsewhere for the signs which are to guide us.

### THE UDDER.

This organ is composed of the mammary glands, and the sac which contains them. The glands themselves should be elastic to pressure, and the skin thin, flexible, and covered with a fine, silky down, mounting to the upper limit of the sac, and extending below towards the navel.

(23)

The udder is furnished with four teats, each of which drains its special reservoir into which the glands empty their secretions. Each of these reservoirs contains a quantity of milk proportioned to its capacity. Although the four reservoirs are closely connected, there is no communication between them, as they are partitioned off from each other by thin, but quite impervious membranes. For this reason a cow can not be thoroughly milked by one or even two teats, but all must be drawn to empty the udder.

A normal udder should give an equal quantity of milk from each teat. The teats themselves should be regular in form, and stand from eight to ten centimetres (about 3 to 4 in.) apart when the udder is full.

The udder of a cow of high order, has, as a rule, but four teats, though occasionally we find two false teats which yield no milk. They are smaller than the proper teats, and are placed behind and a little above the hinder pair. On some cows four false teats are found, symmetrically placed, and very short and small. The false teats are the rudiments of aborted real teats.

Cows of the same breed often present considerable differences in the form of the udder, some having it round, others long and pendant, others again, oblong and compressed, or narrowed in at the middle, while there are cows whose udders resemble that of the goat. In some the teats are very close together, or the front teats are longer and thicker than those behind, while in others the hinder teats are the most developed. Any irregularity in the teats must be looked on as a deformity of greater or less importance, detracting from the value of the animal.

A perfect udder should be of round and regular form, and of volume sufficient to extend beyond the thighs of the animal, nearly as much behind as before.

Those teats which are shorter than the others, denote

some internal alteration, native or acquired, in the teat so dwarfed.

## CUTANEOUS VEINS.

By these I mean those veins on the udder which are seen lying just under the skin. Upon very plump udders they are particularly conspicuous, and when the cow is in full flow of milk, they branch in all directions to the very top of the udder. When the animal is very lean, they may be discerned near the vulva, but they can rarely be seen there if the cow is in good condition. On heifers or dry cows they are not apparent.

## THE MILK-VEINS.

These have their origin in the mammary glands, and run along the lower part of the flank, they extend to a greater or less distance beyond the navel, with various meanderings, and end near the forelegs, their extremities terminating in two cavities commonly called "fountains," the orifice of which is large enough to admit the tip of the finger. In the higher orders of certain breeds these veins end in a net-work of branches. Their extremities are forked, one branch being shorter and thicker than the other.

In some orders the extremities of these veins are about ten centimetres (4 in.) apart, and the calibre of the longer vessel is less than that of the other. In the lower orders these vessels run straight, without sudden and irregular undulations, along each side of the belly; they are not bifurcated, and the pit in which they are lost is smaller and shallower than in the higher orders. These veins are more distinct in some cows than in others of equal milking qualities. Those writers are therefore wrong who attach a high importance to the size and

2

arrangement of these veins as certain indications of a good or bad milker. I have seen many cows in which these veins were far from distinct, which were reputed the best milkers of the neighborhood; while others, which had them highly developed, either gave but little milk or soon went dry. I do not, of course, assert that the indications of these milk-veins have no value at all. I merely wish to impress the fact that we expose ourselves to great errors if we take them as our sole guide in judging the quality of a cow. We often find bastard cows with milk-veins finely developed, and giving a large yield of milk, but which become dry as soon as they are pregnant. I may mention here that the milk-veins do not attain their full development until the cow is five or six years old, and that they are but lightly marked on heifers not with calf.

I shall now proceed to demonstrate that the escutcheon is the only indication that can be relied upon with confidence at all periods of the animal's life, to show its milk-giving qualities with as much certainty as if we had tested them by years of observation.

# CHAPTER III.

## THE ESCUTCHEONS.

Summary.—Escutcheons.—Their number.—What the Escutcheon is.—Its indication.—Variations and precautions.

## ESCUTCHEONS.

In former times men had for their sole guides in determining the qualities of a cow, certain vague physical signs and marks, distributed over various parts of the animal, and giving indications of a very uncertain character. The choice of milch cattle, therefore, was very hazardous, and the most skillful judges, when they saw the certain application of my method, frankly admitted its superiority.

The pretended signs of abundant, persistent, and rich milk, are not only doubtful, but they only appear after the first calving. A young animal must therefore be kept three or four years before its milking qualities can be known, and the choice of heifers for the dairy has hitherto been scarcely more than a matter of chance, so that it constantly happens that the inferior animals are preserved, and those that would turn out good milkers are sent to the butcher.

I affirm with confidence that with a thorough knowledge of my method, any one can distinguish with absolute certainty, during all periods of the animal's life, those cows which will give the most milk, and continue to yield it the longest after another pregnancy has begun. He can even predict the quality of the milk, its richness or poorness in butter, etc.

(27)

The distinctive signs on which my method is founded are called Escutcheons and Feathers (*épis*).\* They exist and may be seen on every animal of the bovine species, without exception. They are situated on the hinder part of the animal, but can not be perfectly distinguished unless the animal walks a few paces, as the movement of walking exhibits the lower part, which cannot be perfectly seen when it is at rest. These signs distinguish the classes, or families, which differ from each other in the form of the escutcheon.

I have not drawn upon the Greek or Latin language for the names which I have given to these escutcheons, preferring to use entirely conventional terms, which, however, have a certain relation to the forms they represent.

### NUMBER OF ESCUTCHEONS.

From years of careful research, and innumerable observations on all breeds of cattle, foreign as well as French, I have determined that there are ten principal forms of escutcheons, each of which is easily distinguished from the others.

### THE ESCUTCHEON.

The surface of the escutcheon is distinguished by its upward-growing hair, which takes a direction opposite to that which covers the other parts of the skin. The hair of the escutcheon is also distinguished by its tint, which is duller than that of the other hair. The escutcheon starts from the middle of the four teats, a part of its hair extending forward under the belly, in the direction of the navel, while the other part, beginning a little above the houghs, spreads as far as the middle of the hinder surface of the thighs, ascending on the udder,

---

\**Epis* means an ear of wheat. I have chosen "Feather" as the best single word in English to represent the form of this mark.—Tr.

and in some classes running up as high as the top of the vulva.

The form or pattern of the escutcheon indicates the class to which the animal belongs, while the extent of surface covered by it denotes the milk-giving capacity. This extent, varying in a decreasing proportion, gives rise to several orders, in which I range the members of each class. The fineness of the hair of the escutcheon, and the color of its skin, indicate the quantity and quality of the milk.

In all the classes and orders the escutcheon is the sole indicator of the internal capacity of the udder, so that if the escutcheon is large, we can pronounce without hesitation that the internal reservoir is large, and the yield of milk will be abundant; while if the escutcheon be small, the reservoir is small, and the yield of milk will be small. Hence those cows which have a large escutcheon, composed of fine hair, are the best milkers, especially if the skin, from the inner joining of the thighs to the vulva, is of a yellowish color, and if on scratching it with the nail we can detach little scales of a fatty substance. Those animals in which this latter characteristic is found in the skin of the switch and of the inside of the ear, yield a milk very rich in butter, whatever be the quantity, and whatever be the class or order to which they belong.

Cows which have the skin of the escutcheon sleek, white, and covered with long, sparse hairs, will give a thin, serous milk; while those whose udder is covered with an escutcheon of short furry hair, will give good and rich milk.

### VARIATIONS AND PRECAUTIONS.

The indications of the escutcheon are often modified, favorably or unfavorably, by various feathers which are pretty generally met with, whose value may be judged

by their form, their character, their situation, and their
size.  Except the Oval feathers, all those which encroach
upon the escutcheon, lessen, in greater or less degree, its
favorable indications.

I must also call special attention to a kind of feather
formed of upward-growing hair, which, by its signification, has a certain likeness to the escutcheon; it is situated on the right and left of the vulva, and its importance varies according to its size and figure.    This
feather, as will be seen, serves to distinguish "free cows"
(*vaches franches, i. e.,* persistent milkers,) from bastards.

By the crossing of classes the patterns of escutcheons
and of feathers are variously modified, as Nature is
always producing new differences.    Crossing either im-
proves or impairs the breed, and its effects influence the
milk-giving and the reproductive functions.    When the
pattern of the escutcheon is true and well-defined, the
animal always belongs to the first or second order of its
class.  But when the escutcheon is invaded by certain
feathers in a portion of its surface, the animal stands one
or more orders lower in its class.

When the escutcheon is wider in the  neighborhood of
the vulva than in its middle part, we must let the widening count against the narrowing, and  obtaining thus an
average width, class the animal in the order which nearest approaches its form and extent.

All variations in the hair of the escutcheon are feathers, constituting an irregularity, and indicating internal
peculiarities which have their influence upon the secretion of milk, and bear relations to the extent of surface
of the feathers.

In general, when we see in an escutcheon a feather
situated to the right or left of the thigh, we may know
that there is an alteration in the milk-vein situated below
it, and by feeling these vessels we shall discover that the
one on the side where the feather encroaches on the

escutcheon, is smaller, and terminates in a smaller cavity than the other vessel, which can easily be verified by introducing the tip of the finger.

When a cow has reached the full term of gestation, a few days before calving, the escutcheon and the feathers enlarge and expand like a flower about to open. The milk-vessels now enlarge, and are in a state to give the maximum of milk a few days after calving, but the escutcheons and feathers soon contract, and assume the size which they will retain until the next calving. It has been noticed that those escutcheons and feathers which have a bristling surface (*hérissés*) attain, just before calving, extraordinary size, often greater by one-third than the ordinary or normal dimensions.

We must therefore be careful not to judge of the yield of milk by the dimensions which the escutcheon assumes at this period, as it would lead us to false conclusions. This great increase in size is due to the functional excitement of the milk-vessels, and the engorgement of the mammary glands; it is more marked in some cows than others, and is always less in the lower orders.

The characteristic signs are indicated by letters in the classification which I shall presently give, in which all the classes and orders are represented with their escutcheons and feathers, drawn from nature, and with their distinguishing variations of form and extent.

Though there is no difficulty in discerning the escutcheons and feathers on animals of any age and in any condition, yet they are more conspicuous on fat animals than on lean ones. When they are thickly covered with fine velvety down, it is not so easy to determine their precise outline without close inspection. This characteristic, however, is a favorable mark.

It sometimes happens, especially in the case of the offspring of parents of different classes, that two forms of escutcheon modify or interpenetrate each other. The primitive type then disappears, and the determination becomes more difficult: we must seek in the two classes to which the parents belong, the orders to which the mixed escutcheon approaches most nearly in form and dimensions, and in this way we can arrive at an approximate estimate.

If we find an escutcheon whose size indicates a cow of the first order, and this escutcheon is accompanied by one or more feathers of upward-growing or downward-growing hair, like those which distinguish the bastards, as this indicates a certain degeneration, the quantity of milk may remain the same, but its persistence will be lessened. According to the nature of these feathers, we may have to go one or more orders lower in the class to determine how long the cow will continue to give milk during her next pregnancy.

On the other hand, if an escutcheon of small dimensions or lower order has the feathers and the fineness of hair which characterize cows of superior quality or higher order, the quantity of milk will not be increased, but it will continue longer during pregnancy, and in this respect the cow of lower order approaches in value an animal of higher order.

GENERAL RULE.—When the marks of an inferior order are superimposed on those of a superior, they indicate a real degeneration; when, on the contrary, the signs designating a superior order are added to those characterizing an inferior, they announce a decided improvement.

Those marks or notches in the escutcheon, in which its ascending is replaced by descending hair, are always the indication of a deterioration proportioned to the size of these notches, and in this case we must rank the cow one or more orders lower in her class to estimate her real value. The same remark applies to breaks in the feathers, caused by a reversal of the hair, and we must take them into account, as they have a marked reference to the quantity and persistence of the milk.

Each of the ten escutcheons which I distinguish, represents a class or family. The first class I term "Flandrine." Second, "Left-hand Flandrine." Third, "Selvedge." Fourth, "Curveline." Fifth, "Bicorn." Sixth, "Double-Selvedge." Seventh, "Demijohn." Eighth, "Square." Ninth, "Limousine." Tenth, "Carresine."

# CHAPTER IV.

## THE FEATHERS.

SUMMARY.—The Feathers.—Nomenclature.—Oval Feather.—Buttock Feather.—Babine Feather.—Vulvous Feather.—Bastard Feather.—Thigh Feather.—Dart Feather.

### THE FEATHERS.

These are of two kinds: those of upward-growing hair, which I call "ascending feathers," and those of downward-growing hair, which I call "descending." The ascending feathers are mere traces in the form of furrows, cutting through the descending hair; they form figures more or less elongated and developed, to the right and left of the vulva, and below it. The descending feathers form designs on the ascending hair of the escutcheon, they have various forms, and especially the Oval. They are mostly situated at the lower part of the udder, a little above the hinder teats.

Each of these feathers, sharply drawn by nature, has, in the form and direction of its hair, a well-defined value and significance.

The feathers are seven in number, of which five are on the escutcheon, and two outside of it. Their significance and importance vary with their extent, the position which they occupy, and the direction of their hair. I had marked these signs in the figures of my first classification, but had not then given them any denomination. Now I have distinguished them by names.

As I have said above, they are seven in number, 1, the "Oval feather." 2, the "Buttock feather." 3, the "Babine feather." 4, the "Vulvous feather." 5, the "Bastard feather." 6, the "Thigh feather." 7, the "Dart feather."

The normal position of these feathers, as of the escutcheon, is on the hinder part of the animal, either on one side, or between the milk producing organs, and those of generation.

### No. 1.—OVAL FEATHER.

This feather is in the escutcheon, on each side of the hinder part of the udder, a little above the two hinder teats; it has an oval form; its hair, fine and "descend-

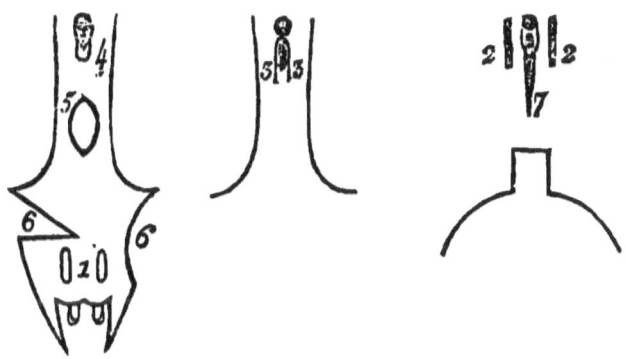

THE FEATHERS.

ing," is distinguished by its tint, and a whiter lustre than that of the escutcheon, which is "ascending." This feather, of greater or less extent, may be found in any of the classes or orders.

In determining the quantity of milk, this feather is of but little importance. Some breeds have the characteristics of the first orders, without the Oval feather, and are none the less excellent milkers. But as a general rule, it is seldom that cows of the higher orders are without it.

If these feathers are small, regular in form, and composed of very fine hair, they are usually an excellent sign, but if large, of irregular shape, and of long and coarse hair, they are a mark of inferior quality.

## No. 2.—BUTTOCK FEATHER.

This feather is outside of the escutcheon, on the buttock of the animal, to the right and left of the vulva, to which it adheres a little at the top. Its hair is ascending, and its proportions are usually from five to seven centimetres (2 to 3 in.) in length, by a centimetre (.4 in.) in breadth.

When the " Buttock feather " does not exceed these proportions, and is covered with a fine silky hair, it indicates the continuance of milk during pregnancy. When it is larger, and covered with coarse and bristling hair, it is not only a mark of inferiority, but indicates the cessation of the milk-flow at an earlier or later period of gestation. These feathers are found on all classes except the first, as may be seen in the figures illustrating my classification.

## No. 3.—BABINE FEATHER.

This feather is rarely met with except in the first two classes. Its place is on the escutcheon, where it forms a vertical streak below the vulva, to the right or left, but most frequently to the left, adhering to the vulva by its upper extremity. It is often found on both sides at once. It is formed of descending hair, and is distinguished by a more shining, or whiter tint than the ascending hair of the escutcheon. Its form is elongated, and its dimensions are variable, but usually from four to five centimetres (1.5 to 2 in.) in length, and five to six millimetres (0.2 to 0.3 in.) in breadth.

The presence of this feather is a mark of degeneration. It indicates a falling-off of milk before and during pregnancy, and this falling-off will be greater in proportion to the size of the feather, and the coarseness of its hair.

## No. 4.—VULVOUS FEATHER.

This is only found in the first class. It is situated in the escutcheon, just beneath the vulva, the lower part of which it encloses. Its form is usually round at the lower part, but sometimes forked. Its dimensions are two centimetres (0.8 in.) in length, by three (1.2 in.) in breadth. Its hair is descending, and it may be distinguished at some distance by its whitish gloss. It indicates a yield of milk less than the normal quantity, especially when it is of larger dimensions than those given, and when its hair is coarse and sparse.

## No. 5.—BASTARD FEATHER.

The Bastard feather presents the form of an egg. Its surface is about ten centimetres (4 in.) in length, by five to eight (2 to 3 in.) in breadth. Its place is in the escutcheon, about twenty centimetres below the vulva. Its descending hair has a whiter gloss than that of the escutcheon around it, which is usually of a somewhat rosy tint.

This feather is found only in the first class (Flandrine,) and denotes a decided falling-off of milk within a few days after impregnation. This falling-off is less considerable when the Bastard feather is small, narrow, and covered with finer hair, but it surely occurs as the animal advances in pregnancy. [See cut on page 50.]

## No. 6.—THIGH FEATHER.

This is usually found on the interior surface of the lower part of the thigh. It encroaches on the escutcheon;

its descending hair forming a re-entering angle, the point of which, sharp or round, extends upon the udder. It is sometimes seen on both thighs, in which case its form is not always regular, but its most usual place is on the right thigh only.

This feather has a whiter gloss than the ascending hair of the escutcheon. It indicates a defect in the secretion of the mammary glands, and a diminution of milk proportioned to its size. It is found in all the classes and orders. As it encroaches upon the escutcheon, it diminishes the surface of the latter in a certain proportion, of which account must be taken in estimating the yield of the cow, as it is equivalent to a descent of one or more orders.

### No. 7.—DART FEATHER.

This feather is distinguished by ascending hair of a soft and silky texture. It resembles a dart or arrow, with the point downward. It starts at about ten centimetres (4 in.) above the escutcheon, and reaches up to the vulva, to which it is attached by a vertical line along the juncture of the buttocks. Its greatest breadth, at the orifice of the vulva, is about 2 centimetres (0.8 in.).

This feather, which indicates the quantity and the persistence of the milk, is but rarely met with, and only in those classes in which the escutcheon does not extend to the vulva. It is represented in a figure placed outside of the classification.

Having now explained the escutcheons and the feathers, that is, all of the signs which indicate milk-giving qualities, I pass to the general classification. This is the practical part of my method, and I have done my best to make it clear and precise, that all may find it easy to apply it.

# CHAPTER V.

## CLASSIFICATION.

## INTRODUCTION.

In studying the classification laid down in this chapter, the reader will observe that animals of the same breed and orders give nearly the same amount of milk, to whatever class they belong. But we must, of course, take into account the size of the animal, whether large, medium, or small, and of its weight.

Nature herself has established the escutcheons; what I have done is to discover their signification and their value. I have divided them into classes and orders corresponding to their figure and dimensions. Had I not proceeded in this manner, the application of my method would have been very difficult. The reader would have been confused by the multiplicity of forms, and the relations of size would have escaped notice, or given very uncertain results. But it must be borne in mind, once for all, that in numbering the classes, first, second, etc., I do not mean thereby to indicate their relative degrees of merit, though it is true that in point of yield of milk there is some difference. The Flandrines, for example, as a class, seem to take the lead; yet this difference is too slight to justify our undervaluing the other classes. All cows of the first order, to whatever class they belong, may be considered as about equal in quality.

In a word, the essential point, in reference both to the

(39)

yield of milk and to the reproduction, is the surface-extent of the escutcheon. But this extent can not be appreciated with sufficient exactness, unless we take into account the form of the escutcheon, co-ordinate it with similar forms, and separate it from the dissimilar. For this reason my classification is absolutely necessary for the proper application of my system. In breeding, the distinction of classes is of still more importance, as there is always an advantage in pairing those animals which have the same pattern of escutcheon.

I might have been asked to fix some positive measure of the surface of the escutcheon, but this I have not attempted, nor would it have been possible, as this surface continually varies with the size, and the fatness or leanness of the animal. But in carefully designating, as I have done, the distances from the outside of the thighs, the houghs, the vulva, etc., to which the margins of the escutcheon should reach—fixing thus the limits of its extreme points—I give the means of distinguishing with precision the order of each.

Those who desire to avoid all mistakes, must do exactly as I do: that is, must descend regularly from order to order of my classification, if they neglect the established orders, and think it unnecessary to follow the regular gradation, they will soon find themselves deceived.

In this new edition of my work, cows are divided into ten classes or families, and each class with six orders. The figures of each order comprise the three degrees of size or stature of each animal. The difference of size does not in any way increase the number of orders, or of classes, for the form of escutcheon is the same on a large animal as a small one, but it will readily be conceived that a cow of large bulk will give more milk, other things being equal, and have greater weight than a small one. If I have made the distinction, it is only with reference to the yield and the weight, and does not affect the difference of the orders.   Upon mature reflection I have determined, for the sake of simplicity, to remove from my classification the last two orders of each class.   I do this because cows of these two orders are rarely met with; but in order that my work may be complete, I place the figures of these orders as an appendix to my regular classification, where they may be found by any one who may chance to meet with animals so marked.

Each class, therefore, consists of six "free" (or legitimate) orders.   The bastards of each class are figured after the orders of their class, and may be recognized by their characteristic feathers.   Their escutcheons being the same as those of "free" cows, I might have avoided the repetition, but as my object is to fix the forms firmly in the memory, I prefer repeating them to leaving any chance of misunderstanding.

And now I repeat, finally, to impress it on the memory, that all cows of every description, "free," or bastard, and all bulls, whatever their size, belong to one or other of the orders of my ten classes or families. Each class has its peculiar escutcheon, and this form is found, with simple modifications of size, in all the orders of the class.

The classes or families of my classification, distinguished by their escutcheons, are as follows:

First Class . . . . . . Flandrine.
Second Class . . . . . Left-hand Flandrine.
Third Class . . . . . . Selvedge.
Fourth Class . . . . . Curveline.
Fifth Class . . . . . . Bicorn.
Sixth Class . . . . . . Double Selvedge.
Seventh Class . . . . Demijohn.
Eighth Class . . . . . Square.
Ninth Class . . . . . Limousine.
Tenth Class . . . . . Carresine.

To give greater clearness to this work, I have illus-

trated it with figures, by the aid of which it will be easy
to recognize the class, the order, and the value of each
cow, and consequently to estimate the quantity of its
daily yield, and the length of time its full flow of milk
will continue after pregnancy.

Frequent experiments have shown that the quantity
and persistence do not always exactly correspond with
the indications, for the reason that differences of climate,
of feeding, and of the season, necessarily have more or
less favorable or unfavorable influence. But in all cases,
the cows of the first orders are the best and most productive, and the yield of milk diminishes in a regular
degree from the highest order to the lowest. Cows of
the seventh and eighth orders, which I have placed
outside of my classification, yield scarcely any milk
at all.

Before entering upon a minute description of each
class, I will recall what has before been said, that every
class has its bastards; that is to say, cows which, although exactly resembling the others in form, size, and
color, differ from them in their yield of milk. This resemblance gives rise to many errors. It is therefore of
great importance to know the characteristic marks by
which the bastards of each class can be recognized.

I have given the name of bastards to those cows which,
on becoming again impregnated, lose their milk immediately, or in a short time. They are found in all classes
and orders: sometimes they are copious milkers, and
their sudden loss of milk after impregnation, has been
referred to various causes, none of which is correct.
This loss is in no wise dependent upon the will of the
animal, as many persons suppose, but is an inborn peculiarity of its constitution. The feathers, or characteristic
marks by which bastards may be distinguished in all the
classes and orders, are described and figured in their
proper places.

As a general rule, these bastards are very fertile, conceiving at the first service of the bull, and if at this time the bastard is suckling a calf, it often happens that she can not supply milk enough for its nourishment. This must be looked to, and the calf promptly weaned, or suckled by another cow. In other respects, such as richness or poorness, abundance or deficiency of milk, the bastards vary, as do the free cows of the different classes and orders.

Cows in general give their maximum of milk in the eight days immediately after calving, but the milk during this period is not suited for human consumption. After this time there is some diminution in its flow, and the normal quantity being established, is maintained until a new impregnation, after which the flow diminishes in all the classes and orders, but more or less according to the class and order, as will be explained more fully.

As I have said, in my introduction, the development which I have given to the escutcheons in the engraved figures, results from my representing them as so many plane surfaces, as if spread out flat. In this way only could the full extent be shown; as it is never shown fully in the animal at rest, and even when the cow is walking, though that movement exhibits it more fully, it still is not entirely displayed.

### FIRST CLASS.—FLANDRINES.

The reader has already been informed that my terminology is by no means scientific or etymological, the names I have chosen for my classes are purely arbitrary. I have called the cows of the first class, which comprises the best animals in our provinces, Flandrines, because the Flanders breed of cows, remarkable for its excellent qualities, usually possesses the signs of this class. The Flandrines are the most abundant milkers of all, they

are found in all breeds, but are of rare occurrence in
some of our provinces. Every order of this class, as of
the others, has certain particular differences in the general characters of the class, and gives a yield varying
according to the degrees which I shall indicate. I call
large cows, those which weigh from three hundred to
three hundred and fifty kilogrammes (say 700 to 800
lbs.). Medium cows, those weighing from two hundred
to two hundred and fifty kilogrammes (say 450 to 550
lbs.). Small cows, those weighing from one hundred
to one hundred and fifty kilogrammes (say 225 to 325 lbs.).

### LARGE COWS.

*First Order.*—Cows of the first order of Flandrines,
of large size, give, when in full flow of milk, twenty-
four litres (25 quarts) daily, up to the time of a new impregnation. From that time there is a gradual diminution; but they continue milking throughout the whole
period of their pregnancy, and if constantly milked,
will never go dry. This, however, should not be done,
as it is important that they should have a rest of a month
or six weeks before calving. Cows of this order, in addition to the characteristic form of the escutcheon, have a
fine elastic udder, covered with a light down, which,
starting from the middle of the four teats, ascends up
the whole surface of the hind part of the animal. This
ascending hair also extends upon the inner side of the
thighs, just above the houghs, and expands to right and
left to the points marked *a, a,* narrowing in again as it
ascends to the points *b, b,* each of which is about ten
centimetres (4 in.) from the corresponding side of
the vulva. They usually have above the two hinder
teats two small Oval feathers of descending hair, marked
*e, e,* each of which is about three centimetres (1.2 in.)
wide, and eight or nine (3.2 or 3.6 in.) long. These

feathers are distinguished by a whiter-colored hair than that of the escutcheon. The first order of this class has, moreover, the inside and lower part of the thighs of a yellowish or nankeen color, speckled with blackish and reddish patches. If we scratch the skin of this part, we detach small scales, from which falls a dust like fine bran, and this, in all the classes, is one of the characteristics denoting a milk rich in butter. All cows having an escutcheon of the form which characterizes the first class, belong to that class, whatever otherwise may

be the dimensions of their escutcheon, their bulk, color, or breed.

At the risk of wearisome repetition, I will once more remind the reader that the escutcheons, as shown in my figures, are not as they are seen in any ordinary posture of the animal, but spread out as if the skin were removed and extended over a plane surface, so as to exhibit their full size and configuration.

*Second Order.*—Cows of this order in full milking will give twenty litres (21 quarts) of milk a day, and will continue this quantity until they are seven months gone with calf. The marks of this order perfectly coincide with those of the first order, and I have indicated them by the same letters. They have, besides, a little feather

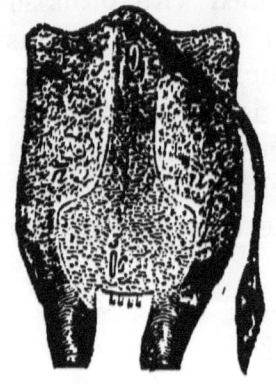

of descending hair, which I call the "Babine Feather," placed below and to one side of the vulva, or often on both sides at once. This feather is indicated by the letter *f*. It measures about six centimetres (2.4 in.) in length, by about one (0.4 in.) in breadth. It is distinguished by very short hair, and indicates an inferiority in the daily milking amounting to two or even three litres (2 or 3 quarts). This order has but a single Oval feather above the teats, measuring six centimetres (2.4 in.) in length, by three (1.2 in.) in breadth.

*Third Order.*—Cows of this order give sixteen litres (17 quarts) of milk daily, and continue milking until they are six months gone with calf. The form of the escutcheon is similar to that of the preceding order, but

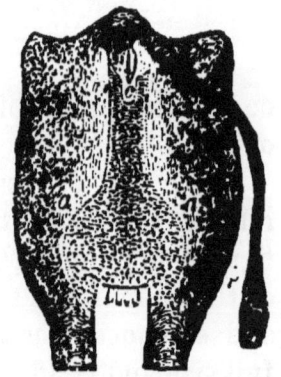

narrower; and as another difference, it has a feather which I call the "Vulvous Feather," forming a semicircle of descending hair under the vulva, extending upwards, so as to inclose it in a fork, spreading from two to three centimetres (0.8 to 1.2 in.) with a length of about the same. This mark is indicated by the letter *c;* it is distinguished by a whiter color than the ascending hair. This order has sometimes an Oval feather to the left, above the hinder teats.

*Fourth Order.*—Cows of the fourth order, when in

full milking, give twelve litres (12'/₂ quarts) daily, and continue this quantity until they are five months gone with calf. The escutcheon of this order differs from the preceding by the smaller surface of the ascending hair. The points *a, a,* are withdrawn more within the thighs. The points *b, b,* are nearer the vulva, and the Vulvous feather of descending hair is found embracing the vulva, with a form often rounded at the base, and sometimes terminating in a fork. This feather is larger than that in the preceding order, marked *c,* and it is also dis-

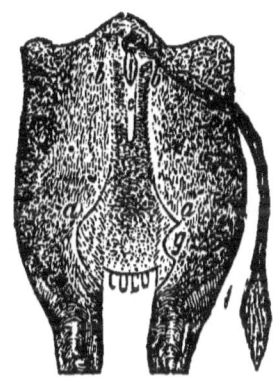

tinguished by hair of still whiter lustre. There is no Oval feather to the right of the escutcheon, but there is a "Thigh feather," marked *g.*

*Fifth Order.*—Cows of the fifth order give nine litres (9'/₂ quarts) of milk daily, and continue milking until four months gone with calf. The escutcheon of this order is a little more narrowed in at the points *a, a,* and b, b, than in the preceding order; beneath the vulva is a feather forming a line of descending hair of about fifteen centimetres (6 in.) long, by three (1.2 in.) wide, indicated on the figure by the letter *c.* To the right is a Thigh feather of descending hair, which encroaches on the escutcheon in the part which is hidden between the thighs. It is about fifteen centimetres (6 in.)

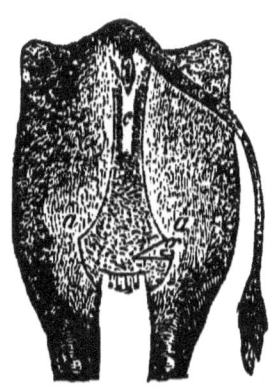

deep, by eight or ten (3.2 or 4 in.) wide, and is indicated by the letter *g.*

*Sixth Order.*—Cows of this order give six litres (6 quarts) of milk daily, and continue this quantity until they are three months gone with calf. The escutcheon is still more contracted at the points *a*, *a*, than in the preceding order, and the Vulvous feather is larger. Some-

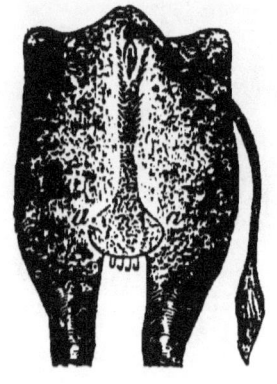

times two Thigh feathers of descending hair are found, making two notches in the escutcheon. The feathers found in this escutcheon distinguish the degenerate varieties.

In the preceding descriptions I have spoken of animals of large size, and to those alone do the statements of milk-yield apply. For animals of less size there is no need that I should describe the escutcheons and feathers, those signs being the same on large or small animals, but I will give in condensed form a statement of the daily yield of milk, and its continuance after impregnation.

### MEDIUM SIZE.

*First Order.*—Cows of this order, in full milking, give nineteen litres (20 quarts) daily, and continue it, like those of large size, during the whole period of gestation. They may be milked down to the very time of their calving. On all these points they exactly resemble those of large size.

*Second Order.*—These give fifteen litres (16 quarts) of milk daily, and continue it until seven months gone with calf.

*Third Order.*—Twelve litres (12¹/₂ quarts) of milk daily, continued until six months gone with calf.

*Fourth Order.*—Nine litres (9¹/₂ quarts) daily, until five months gone with calf.

*Fifth Order.*—Six litres (6 quarts) daily, until four months gone with calf.

*Sixth Order.*—Three litres (3 quarts) daily, until three months gone with calf.

SMALL SIZE.

*First Order.*—Cows of small size of the first order give, when in full flow of milk, fourteen litres (15 quarts) daily, and keep it up for eight months.

*Second Order.*—Eleven litres ($11^1/_2$ quarts) daily, until seven months gone with calf.

*Third Order.*—Eight litres (8 quarts) daily, until six months gone with calf.

*Fourth Order.*—Six litres (6 quarts) daily, until five months gone with calf.

*Fifth Order.*—Three litres (3 quarts) daily, until four months gone with calf.

*Sixth Order.*—One litre (1 quart) daily, until three months gone with calf.

## BASTARDS BELONGING TO THE CLASS OF FLANDRINES.

To preserve the connection of my arrangement, I append to each class a description of the bastards that belong to it. I now proceed to describe the bastards of the Flandrines, reminding the reader that this description applies to cows of all sizes.

These cows being met with in all the orders of this class, to estimate correctly their yield of milk, we must proceed as with "free" cows; that is, adding to, or taking from, the normal yield, as indicated by the form and dimensions of their escutcheons.

Flandrine cows have two species of bastards. The first —No. 1—has the Bastard feather marked *j*, in the figure. Its hair is descending, and it is placed high up in the median line of the escutcheon. Its form is oval, and its

3

distance below the vulva about two decimetres (8 in.)
This feather is from ten to twelve centimetres (4 to 4.8
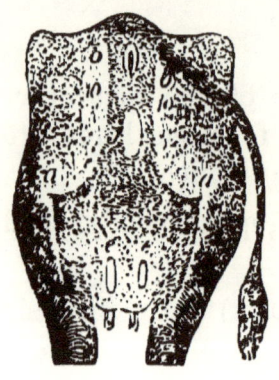 in.) in length, to from six to seven
(2.4 to 2.8 in.) in breadth. It shows
of a whiter gloss than the escutcheon. The larger this feather, the
more rapid is the falling-off in milk,
if it is small, the loss is less considerable, but it certainly occurs as
the animal advances in pregnancy.
The presence of this feather is
the only mark by which we can
distinguish the bastards of this
kind (No. 1,) from the free orders.

The bastard No. 2, has the same characteristics as the
" free " cows of the first order of the class. The escutcheon is the same; only, instead of ascending vertically towards the vulva, the hair of its margins spreads sideways
over the thighs and buttocks of the animal, flaring out
like an ear of wheat. On the inside of the thighs, as far
as the vulva, the skin is delicate and of a reddish color,
but no fine scales detach themselves from it, as in the
first orders. The largest escutcheons, of the finest hair,
are those which indicate the most abundant supply of
milk. When the hair is coarse, long, and transparent, it
is a sign of poor milk. The description of this variety
of bastards being sufficiently explicit, I have not thought
it necessary to illustrate it by a special figure.*

SECOND CLASS.—LEFT-HAND FLANDRINES.

I have given the name of Left-hand Flandrines to this
class, because it presents on the left-side, the character-

*In order not to multiply the number of figures, I have represented
the bastards of each class with the escutcheons of the first orders.
When the classification is consulted for bastards of other orders, the
bastardy may be referred to the figures representing the corresponding
orders of " free " cows.

istics of the Flandrines just described. In this class, as in the others, the cows which are characterized by the escutcheons indicated in the designs of the class, are all considered as belonging to the same family.

*First Order.*—Cows of the first order of this class, give, when in full flow of milk, twenty-two litres (23 quarts) daily, and continue milking, with a continually

lessening supply, until they are eight months gone with calf. Like the cows of the first order of the first class, they will never go dry if constantly milked. Those of the first order have a fine udder covered with soft down, which ascends from the middle of the four teats, spreads within and a little above the houghs, and extends over the thighs to the points marked *a, a.* The right side of the escutcheon is checked by a transverse line, running toward the center of the thighs. The left side rises in a vertical line as high as the top of the vulva, where the escutcheon ends with a breadth of about eight to ten centimetres (3 to 4 in.) at the point *b.*

Above the hinder teats, as in the first order of the first class, we find two Oval feathers of descending hair, marked *e, e*, being each four to five centimetres (1.6 to 2 in.) in breadth, by eight to ten (3 to 4 in.) in length, and conspicuous by the whiter lustre of the hair. The first order of this class, moreover, like that of the preceding, has the inside of the thighs and perinæum, as high as the vulva, of a yellowish or nankeen color,

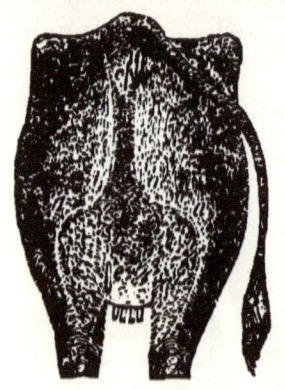

sprinkled with black and red spots; and on scratching the skin with the nail, small unctuous scales are detached like fine bran, or the powder of some fatty substance.

*Second Order.*—These cows give eighteen litres (19 quarts) milk daily, and continue until they are seven months gone with calf. The pattern of the escutcheon is the same as that of the first order; but the points *a, a*, are nearer together, and the whole figure is narrowed. It has on the left of the vulva, a Babine feather of descending hair, marked *c*, in the figure, of six to seven centimetres (2.4 to 2.8 in.) in length, by one in breadth. The whole escutcheon is distinguished by the gloss of its reversed hair; there is but a single oval feather above the teats, which is situated on the left of the udder, and marked *e* in the figure.

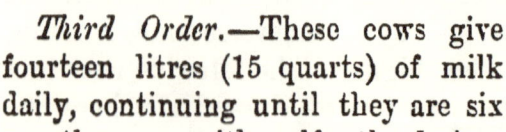

*Third Order.*—These cows give fourteen litres (15 quarts) of milk daily, continuing until they are six months gone with calf; the design of the escutcheon is the same as in the first and second orders, but still more contracted. The points *a*, *a*, are lower and nearer together. To the left of the vulva may be seen a white streak in the ascending hair; this is the Babine feather of descending hair, marked in the figure by *c;* it is from twelve to fifteen centimetres (4.8 to 6 in.) long, by two (0.8 in.) broad.

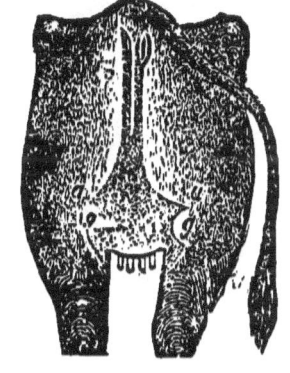

*Fourth Order.* — Cows of this order give ten litres (10'/₂ quarts) of milk daily, and continue it until they are five months gone with calf. They have the same upper mark as the preceding order; the lines of the escutcheon run nearer together, and the whole figure is more contracted. The points *a*, *a*, are lower and less extended; the Babine feather, *c*, to the left of the vulva, is of descending hair, longer and wider than that of the preceding order. Beneath the points *a*, *a*, to the left or right, sometimes appears the Thigh feather *g*, formed of descending hair, forming a continuation of that of the thighs, and encroaching on the escutcheon. All the orders of this class may have this feather, which is always indicative of a smaller yield of milk.

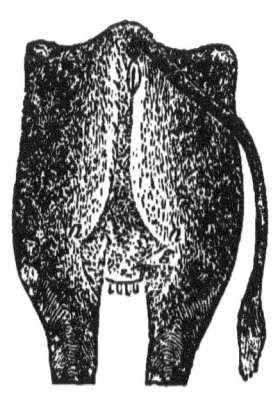

*Fifth Order.*—Cows of this order give seven litres (7 quarts) of milk daily, continuing it until they are four months gone with calf. The escutcheon is more contracted than in the preceding order; on the left side, the hair, instead of ascending vertically, feathers out sideways like the beard of an ear of wheat; the hair, coarser over all the escutcheon, is irregular on the right side, from the presence of the

Thigh feather, *g*, which replaces a part of the ascending, by descending hair. This feather begins on the inner surface of the thigh, and is lost on the surface of the udder.

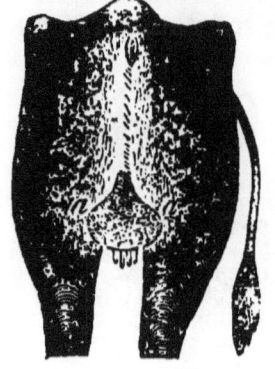

*Sixth Order.*—Cows of this order give four litres (4 quarts) of milk daily, and continue only three months after a new impregnation. The pattern of the escutcheon is narrower than the preceding; and the upper part is formed of coarse hairs, feathering off to the left.

### MEDIUM SIZE.

*First Order.*—Cows of medium size of the first order, give, when in full milking, seventeen litres (18 quarts) daily, continuing it for eight months after impregnation, like those of large size. Like those, also, they can be milked down to the very time of calving.

*Second Order.*—These give fourteen litres (15 quarts) of milk daily, continued until they are seven months gone with calf.

*Third Order.*—Ten litres (10$\frac{1}{2}$ quarts) of milk daily, continued until they are six months gone with calf.

*Fourth Order.*—Seven litres (7 quarts) of milk daily, continued until they are five months gone with calf.

*Fifth Order.*—Four litres (4 quarts) of milk daily, continued until they are four months gone with calf.

*Sixth Order.*—Two litres (2 quarts) of milk daily, continued until they are three months gone with calf.

## SMALL SIZE.

*First Order.*—Cows of this order, in full milking, give twelve litres (12¹/₂ quarts) of milk daily, and continue it as do those of large and medium size, the quantity diminishing gradually as their pregnancy advances.

*Second Order.*—Ten litres (10¹/₂ quarts) of milk daily, continued until they are seven months gone with calf.

*Third Order.*—Seven litres (7 quarts) daily, until six months gone with calf.

*Fourth Order.*—Four litres (4 quarts) daily, until five months gone with calf.

*Fifth Order.*—Two litres (2 quarts) daily, until four months gone with calf.

*Sixth Order.*—One litre (1 quart) daily, until three months gone with calf.

### BASTARD LEFT-HAND FLANDRINES.

The bastards of this class are distinguished by a peculiarity in the escutcheon, which takes a large and irregular development in the upper part and 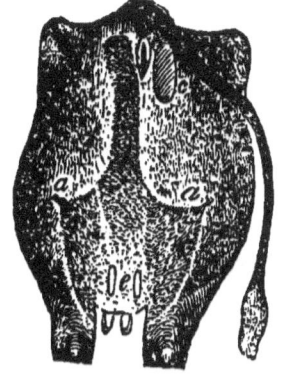 to the left of the vulva, and the hair is also bristling. In addition we shall find the Buttock feather, situated to the right of the vulva, with which it is almost in contact; it is marked *c* in the figure. This feather, the hair of which grows almost horizontally, is about twelve to fifteen centimetres (4.8 to 6 in.) in length, by seven to eight (2.8 to 3.2 in.) in breadth. The smaller this feather is, the less diminution of milk does it indicate, but none the less the cows marked with it lose their milk gradually, after a new impregnation.

### THIRD CLASS.—SELVEDGE COWS.

The form of the escutcheon of this class is very different from that of the two preceding. Its ascending part is formed by a streak of upward-growing hair in the form of a selvedge or list, extending upward vertically, and ending at the vulva without any interruption.

#### LARGE SIZE.

*First Order.*—The large cows of the first order of this class, give twenty-four litres (25 quarts) of milk daily,

and continue it until they are eight months gone with calf, or even until calving, if the milking is kept up. They have a fine, elastic, and velvety udder, covered with a light ascending down. The escutcheon starts from the middle of the four teats, extends within the thighs and above the houghs, spreading out to the points *a, a,* from which points, two transverse horizontal lines run in toward the joining of the thighs, as far as the points *b, b,* which are about ten centimetres (4 in.) apart. A double line starting from the points *b, b,* mounts vertically to the vulva, where the escutcheon ends with a breadth of two centimetres (0.8 in.) Above the two hinder teats, are two Oval feathers, *e, e,* of ascending hair, which are very nearly as large as those described in the first order of Flandrines; they are distinguished by a whiter color than that of the escutcheon. In the first order of Selvedge cows, as in the first order of Flandrines, the color of the escutcheon from the junction of the thighs, is of a yellowish, or nankeen tint, as high as the vulva.

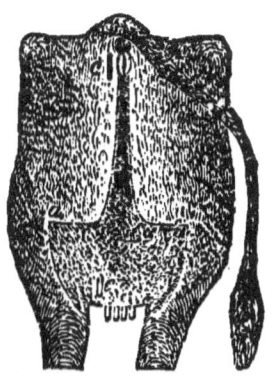

*Second Order.*—These cows give twenty litres (21 quarts) of milk daily, and continue it until they are seven months gone with calf. Their escutcheon has the same form as that of the first order; the points *a, a,* are nearer together, however, and the whole figure is more contracted. There is a Buttock

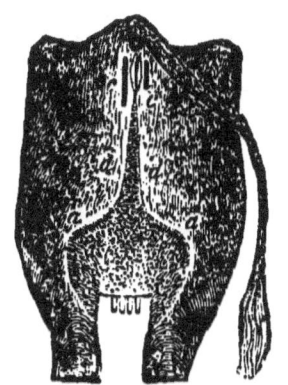

feather, *c,* of ascending hair to the left of the vulva; it is about four centimetres (1.6 in.) long, by about one centimetre (0.4 in.) wide, and is distinguished by the whitish lustre of the reversed hair. Above the teats is a single Oval feather, marked *e.*

*Third Order.*—Cows of this order give sixteen litres (17 quarts) of milk daily, and continue it until they are six months gone with calf. The marks of this order are nearly the same as those of the preceding order, but the points *a*, *a*, are closer together and lower. The escutcheon terminates at the vulva by a sharp point, to the right

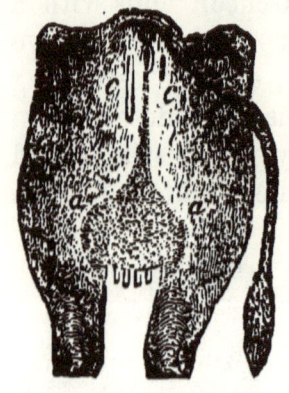

and left of which are two Buttock feathers of ascending hair, *c*, *c*, of the same breadth as that of the preceding order; but the right one is several centimetres shorter than the left.

*Fourth Order.*—Cows of this order give twelve litres (12$\frac{1}{2}$ quarts) of milk daily, and continue it until they are five months gone with calf. The escutcheon is more contracted than in the preceding order, the points *a*, *a*, are closer together, standing not more than two decimetres (8 in.) apart; the list or stripe ascends as high as the vulva, where it terminates in a sharp point. To right and left of the vulva, there are two Buttock feathers, marked *c;* they are wider and longer than in the preceding order.

*Fifth Order.*—Cows of this order give nine litres (9$\frac{1}{2}$ quarts) of milk daily, and continue it until they are four months gone with calf. The escutcheon is still more contracted, the ascending line is very slender, and is broken in the

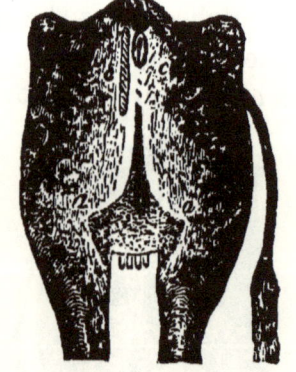

upper half, with interspaces of one, two, or three centimetres. The Buttock feathers, *c*, *c*, are longer and wider than those of the preceding order.

*Sixth Order.*—Cows of this order give six litres (6 quarts) of milk daily, ceasing when they are three months gone with calf. The escutcheon is even more contracted, and the ascending line is broken by wider intervals than in the preceding order. Buttock feathers are often found to right and left of the vulva, in which they are longer and broader, and of coarser and more bristly hair, than in the preceding order.

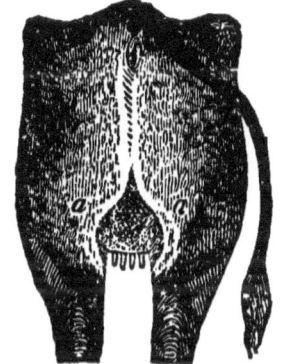

### MEDIUM SIZE.

*First Order.*—Cows of this size and order, give, when in full milking, nineteen litres (20 quarts) daily, and continue until they are eight months gone with calf.

*Second Order.*—Fifteen litres (16 quarts,) continued until they are seven months gone with calf.

*Third Order.*—Twelve litres ($12^1/_2$ quarts,) continued until six months in calf.

*Fourth Order.*—Nine litres ($9^1/_2$ quarts,) continued until five months gone with calf.

*Fifth Order.*—Six litres (6 quarts,) continued until four months gone with calf.

*Sixth Order.*—Three litres (3 quarts,) continued until three months gone with calf.

### SMALL SIZE.

The yield of the cows of small size, is the same in quantity and continuance, as that of the Flandrines of the same size and order.

## BASTARD SELVEDGE COWS.

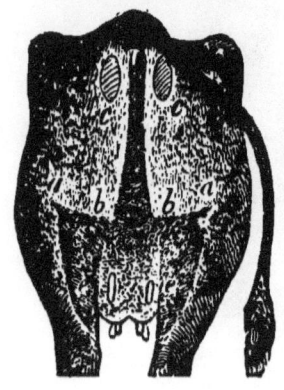

The bastards of this class, of every size and order, may be recognized by two Buttock feathers, one on each side at the height of the vulva. These feathers are from ten to twelve centimetres (4 to 4.8 in.) long, by from four to six (1.6 to 2.4 in.) wide. When these feathers are pointed at the extremities, and of a coarse hair, they indicate a thin and watery milk. But whatever their form, they are a sign of an early loss of milk after impregnation.

## FOURTH CLASS.—CURVELINES.

I have applied this name to cows of the fourth class, because the outline of their escutcheon, which is somewhat of a lozenge shape, is formed by curved lines starting from the right and left, and ascending until they join at about five to six centimetres (2 to 2.4 in.) below the vulva. This class is very abundant in milk, in which respect it approaches the first. Cows of this class are found in all breeds, the production varying with the size and order, as in the previous classes.

### LARGE SIZE.

*First Order.*—Cows of this size and order, give, when in full milking, twenty-four litres (25 quarts) of milk daily, and continue, but with a gradual diminution, until they are eight months gone with calf. The skin of the escutcheon is covered with the same saffron-yellow pellicles, and the same fine down, as that of cows of the first order of the preceding classes. The escutcheon widens more at the top, starting from between the four teats, within and above the houghs, it ascends, spreading to right and left, as high as the middle of the thighs, at the points *a, a.* From these points start, to right and left, two curved lines, concave inwardly, which end at the point *b,* about four or five centimetres (1.6 or 2 in.) from the vulva. Above and opposite the hinder teats,

there are, as in cows of the first order, of the preceding classes, two Oval feathers of descending hair, marked *e, e.* Cows of the first order of this class, may have the Buttock feathers to right and left of the vulva. When these exist, their length is from three to four centimetres (1.2 to 1.6 in.), and their breadth one. They denote the continuance of milk during pregnancy, though it frequently happens that cows which are destitute of these feathers preserve their milk equally well.

*Second Order.*—Cows of this order give twenty litres

(21 quarts) of milk daily, continuing until they are seven

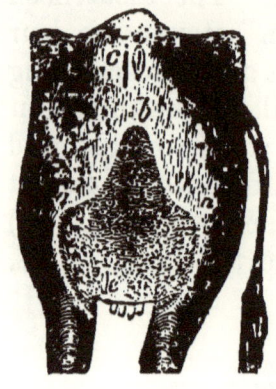

months gone with calf. The form of the escutcheon is the same as in the preceding order, but rather more contracted in all its parts. To the left of the vulva is seen a Buttock feather of ascending hair, marked c, about four centimetres (1.6 in.) long by one (0.4 in.) wide. In this order there is but one Oval feather, e, on the left side, above the teats.

*Third Order.*—Cows of this order give sixteen litres (17 quarts) of milk daily, continuing until they are eight months gone with calf. The pattern of the escutcheon is more contracted than in the preceding order, but resembles it in form. To right and left of the vulva are two Buttock feathers of ascending hair, marked c, c, of about a decimetre (4 in.) in length by two centimetres (0.8 in.) in width. Above the teats on the

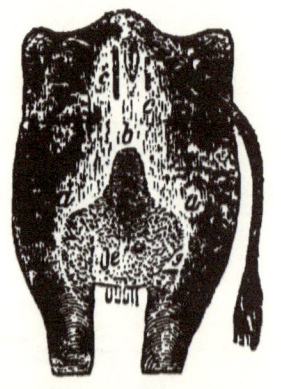

left side there is an Oval feather, marked e; the point,

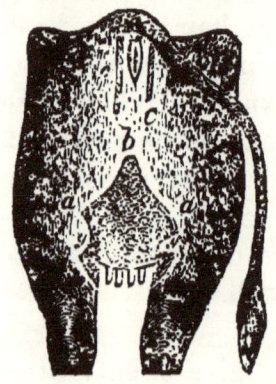

b, is lower than in the preceding order, and to the right, below the letter a, may be noticed a feather of descending hair, making a notch in the escutcheon.

*Fourth Order.*—Cows of this order give twelve litres (12¹/₂ quarts) of milk daily, and cease milking when they are five months gone with calf. The escutcheon is lower and still more contracted; the Buttock feather, *c*, is seen on each side of the vulva. It is fifteen centimetres (6 in.) long by three (1.2 in.) wide, the one on the right is shorter than the other. Below the points, *a, a*, to right and left of the thighs, appear the thigh feathers, *g, g*, of about ten centimetres (4 in.) wide by about fifteen (6 in) long.

*Fifth Order.*—Cows of this order give nine litres ($9^1/_2$ quarts) of milk daily, and cease milking when they are four months gone with calf. The escutcheon is still more contracted in all its parts, the buttock and thigh feathers are longer and wider than in the preceding order.

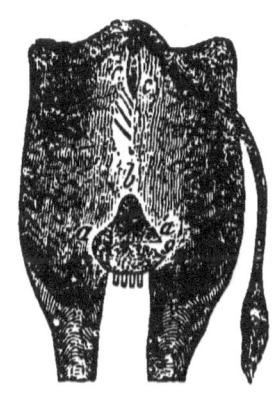

*Sixth Order.*—Cows of this order give six litres (6 quarts) of milk daily, and cease milking when three months gone with calf. Though the escutcheon shows the distinctive form of the class, it is so small as to be scarcely appreciable, and indicates a very poor milker.

### MEDIUM SIZE.

The yield of cows of this size is the same in quantity and continuance as that of Flandrines of the same size and order.

### SMALL SIZE.

Same as for Flandrines of the same size and order.

REMARK.—In this class the detached feathers to right and left of the vulva, marked *c, c*, should be carefully observed. To be a favorable sign, they should have exactly the size indicated in the description of the characteristics of each order.

## BASTARDS.

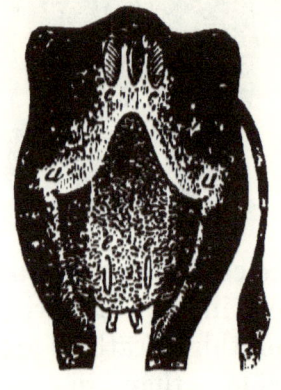

When the Buttock feathers are of a length of ten to twelve centimetres (4 to 4.8 in.), with a width of six to eight (2.4 to 3.2 in.), ending in a point at each extremity, and of coarse, rough hair, they denote a bastard, who will lose her milk as soon as she is again impregnated, or very shortly after.

## FIFTH CLASS.—BICORNS.

I give this name to the cows of my fifth class, because their escutcheon is bifurcated, and resembles two ascending horns, that on the left being longer than the other. Cows of this class are productive, and copious milkers. This class is found in all our breeds. Each order, as in the other classes, has some difference in the details of the characteristic signs. The yield, as in other cases, is in proportion to the size and the order.

### LARGE SIZE.

*First Order.*—Cows of this class and order give, when in full flow of milk, twenty-four litres (25 quarts) daily, and continue until they are eight months gone with calf. The hair of the escutcheon in the first order of this class, has the fineness of that in the preceding orders. The

udder is covered with a fine down, and small scales of a
saffron-color may be detached from the interior of the
thighs, as high as the vulva. The escutcheon, as stated
above, has two ascending horns, ending at a distance of
about a decimetre (4 in.) from the vulva, while the
middle portion dips, as is shown at *o*. The escutcheon,
as in the previous classes, starts from the middle of the
four teats, inside and above the houghs, with ascending
hair over all its surface; it spreads over upon the thighs

at the points *a, a,* and starting from these points, its
outline describes a curve, rising to the points *b, b,* when
it dips inward again to the point *o*. On the sides of the
vulva are two Buttock feathers of ascending hair, marked
*c, c,* of about five centimetres (2 in.) in length, by about
one (0.4 in.) in width. Above the two hinder teats, are
two Oval feathers, *e, e,* as in the first orders of the preceding classes.

*Second Order.*—Cows of this order give twenty litres
(21 quarts) of milk daily, continuing until they are seven
months gone with calf. The escutcheon has the same

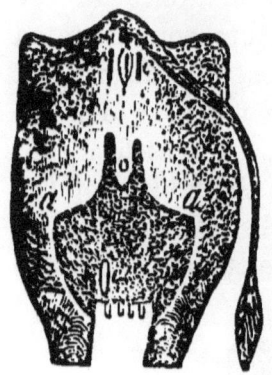

form as in the preceding order, but is lower and more contracted. The color of the pellicles is the same. Of the two Buttock feathers to right and left of the vulva, that on the left is the longer, measuring about eight centimetres (3.2 in.), by one and a half (0.6 in.), that on the right measuring about six centimetres (2.4 in.) by one (0.4 in.) The right horn of the escutcheon is also lower, by one or two centimetres (0.4 or 0.8 in.) than the left. There is but a single oval feather, *e*, on the left above the teats.

*Third Order.*—Cows of this order give sixteen litres (17 quarts) of milk daily, continuing until they are six months gone with calf. The escutcheon is still lower than in the second order; there are two Buttock feathers to right and left of the vulva, somewhat longer and wider than in the preceding order. The

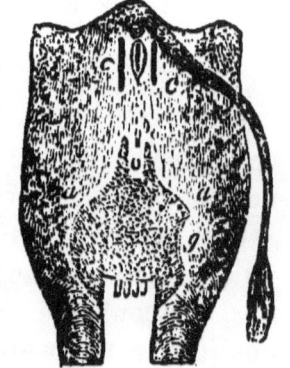

right horn of the escutcheon is from two to three centimetres (0.8 to 1.2 in.) lower than the left. There is no Oval feather above the teats. Beneath the point *a*, on the right side, may be observed an encroachment of descending hair, from that of the thigh, distinguishable from the ascending hair of the escutcheon by its whiter color. The more extensive this patch of descending hair, the less will be the yield of milk.

*Fourth Order.*—Cows of this order give twelve litres (12¹/₂ quarts) of milk daily, continuing until they are five months gone with calf. The escutcheon has the same form, but is more contracted, and further from the vulva. Beneath the point *a*, on the right, is a notch or gore of descending hair, forming an acute angle, marked *g*, which almost divides the escutcheon. To right and left of the vulva, at the points *c, c*, are two Buttock feathers of ascending, and bristling hair; that on the left measures about twelve centimetres (4.8 in.) long, by about two or three (0.8 or 1.2 in.) wide; that on the

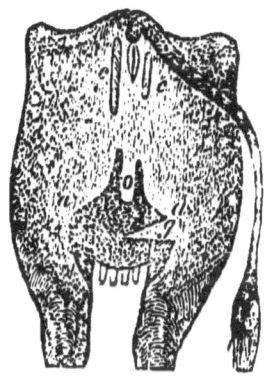

right is from eight to ten centimetres (3.2 to 4 in. long,) by two or three wide.

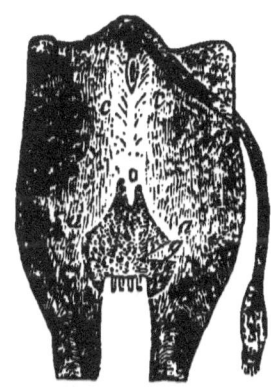

*Fifth Order.*—Cows of this order give nine litres (9$^1/_2$ quarts) of milk daily, continuing until four months gone with calf. The escutcheon is still lower, and more withdrawn into the junction of the thighs, the horns are diminished in length. To right and left of the vulva are two Buttock feathers of ascending and bristly hairs; that on the right is the smaller. On the right side of the escutcheon will be found the Thigh feather, *g.*

*Sixth Order.*—Cows of this order give six litres (6 quarts) of milk daily, until three months gone with calf. The escutcheon is still smaller than in the fifth order, the ascending hairs to the left of the vulva are more spread out, and quite bristling. Cows of this order are poor milkers, and can scarcely nourish their calves.

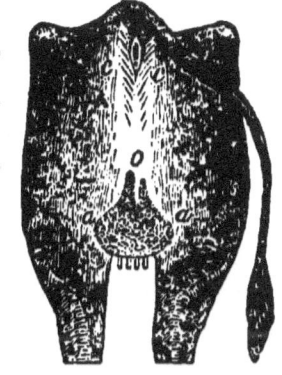

## MEDIUM SIZE.

The yield of cows of this size is the same, both as to quantity and persistence, as that of Flandrines of the same size and order.

## SMALL SIZE.

The same as for Flandrines of the same size and order.

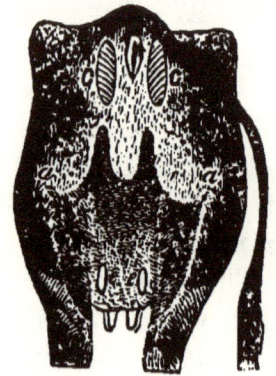

## BASTARDS.

The bastards of Bicorn cows can be recognized by the Buttock feathers, $c$, $c$, being much longer and wider than those of the "free" cows. These cows give a liberal supply of milk, but their milk fails as soon as they are again with calf.

## SIXTH CLASS.—DOUBLE SELVEDGE COWS.

The name which I have given this new class is purely arbitrary, and was suggested by the odd appearance of the escutcheon. The escutcheon of Double Selvedge Cows, differs from that of the third or Selvedge class, by being divided throughout its whole length, into two equal parts by a band of descending hair. This band, of from eight to ten centimetres (3.2 to 4 in.) in width, surrounds the vulva, and descends to the point $j$, near the hinder teats. It is bordered on each side throughout its whole length, and at its extremity by a double fillet, $c$, $c$, of ascending hair, of about two centimetres (0.8 in.) in width, which fillet is, in fact, a prolongation of the escutcheon, in the direction of the vulva. This escutcheon, like those of the other classes, starts from the middle of the four teats, within and above the houghs, and spreads out to the points *a, a,* where it is bordered by two horizontal lines; thence running in to the points *b, b,* from which it is continued by the ascending fillets *c, c,* and ends above on each side of the vulva.

LARGE SIZE.

*First Order.*—Cows of this order and size give twenty-two litres (23 quarts) of milk daily, continuing it, but with a progressive diminution during gestation, until

they are eight months gone with calf, and if constantly milked, will never go dry. The cows of this first order have the udder fine, elastic, and covered with a silky down. The skin of the escutcheon is of a yellowish, or nankeen color.

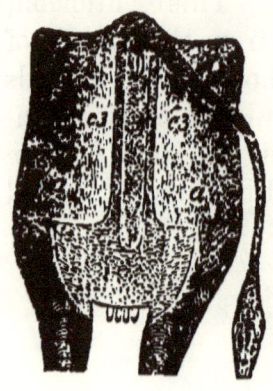

*Second Order.*—Cows of the second order give eighteen litres (19 quarts) of milk daily, continuing until they are seven months gone with calf. Their escutcheon is of the same form as that of the preceding order, but a little narrower in surface. The descending band of hair, marked *j*, ends about eight to ten centimetres (3.2 to 4 in.) above the teats.

*Third Order.*—Cows of this order, when in full flow of milk, give fourteen litres (15 quarts) of milk daily, continuing until they are six months gone with calf. The escutcheon has the same form as in the preceding orders, but is still more contracted; the two fillets are narrower by half at the top than in the first order, and the central band of descending hair ends near the center of the udder, about fifteen centimetres (6 in.) above the hinder teats.

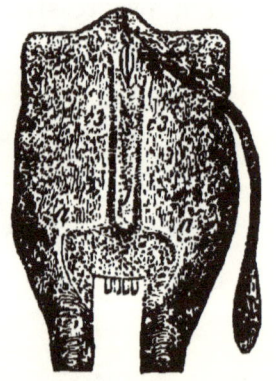

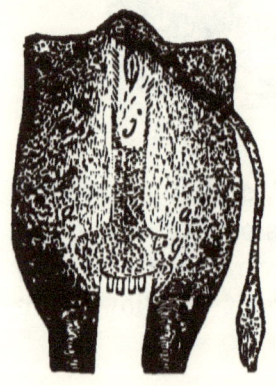

*Fourth Order.*—Cows of this order give ten litres (10$^1/_2$ quarts) of milk daily, and cease milking when five months gone with calf. The escutcheon resembles the preceding, but the two fillets which ascend toward the vulva, are still narrower and closer together, their distance apart being from five to six centimetres. The hair is coarser and denser; the central part, of descending hair, marked *j*, is only about three decimetres (12 in.) in length. Beneath the letter *a*, on the right of the escutcheon, is a Thigh feather, marked *g*.

*Fifth Order.*—Cows of this order give seven litres (7 quarts) of milk daily, and cease milking when they are four months gone with calf. The escutcheon is more contracted than in the preceding orders, the descending band of hair ends at from two to three centimetres (0.8 to 1.2 in.) above the udder. The hair of the escutcheon is denser and more bristling than in the preceding orders, and there are two Thigh feathers, marked *g*.

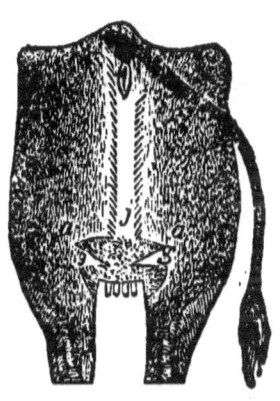

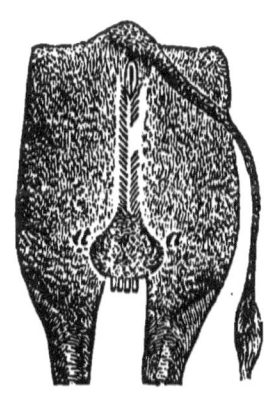

*Sixth Order.*—Cows of this order give four litres (4 quarts) of milk daily, and cease milking when three months gone with calf. The escutcheon is greatly withdrawn within the thighs, the two fillets of ascending hair are very near together, and vanish before reaching the vulva. That of the right is much shorter than the left. This escutcheon indicates an exceedingly small yield of milk.

### MEDIUM SIZE.

The yield of cows of medium size is the same, as to quantity and continuance, as that of Left-hand Flandrines of the same size and order.

### SMALL SIZE.

The same as for Left-hand Flandrines of the same size and order.

### BASTARDS.

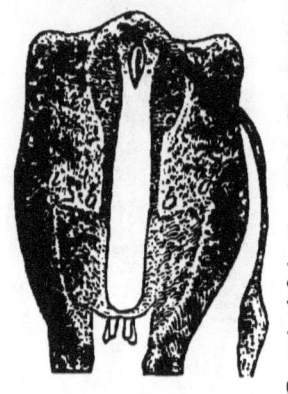

Bastards of this class are recognizable by the two But-tock feathers, one on the right and the other on the left of the vulva. These feathers are from ten to twelve centimetres (4 to 4.8 in.) long by seven or eight (2.8 or 3.2 in.) wide. The two fillets ascend as high as the Buttock feathers, which they join, especially on the right side; these feathers are formed of coarse, bristling hair. The larger the es-cutcheon and the smaller the feath-ers, the better is the cow, and the longer will she continue milking.

### SEVENTH CLASS.—DEMIJOHNS.

The name of this class has been given from the resem-blance of the form of the escutcheon to that of a demijohn.*

#### LARGE SIZE.

*First Order.*—Cows of this size and order give, when in full milking, twenty-four litres (25 quarts) of milk daily, continuing until they are eight months gone with calf. The first order of this class has the skin of the escutcheon of the same color as that of the first orders of the preceding classes; the udder is fine, and covered with a silky down on the interior of the thighs, the small pellicles which may be detached from the epidermis

---

* The name given by M. Guenon is " Poitevines," a term which, as he explains, has no reference to the cows of Poitou, but is a word of his own coinage, derived from wine-jug (*pot de vin*), or demijohn. As the term " Demijohn " has been used by previous writers in this country, it has been retained here.—TR.

are unctuous to the touch. The escutcheon starts from the middle of the four teats, within and above the houghs, spreads toward the middle of the thigh at the points *a, a,* whence proceed two transverse re-entering lines, reaching to the points *j, j,* situated about twelve to fifteen centimetres (4.8 to 6 in.) apart; from these latter points a double line of ascending hair is prolonged upward, terminating squarely at *n.* This part is from six to eight centimetres (2.4 to 3.2 in.) wide, and stops

at about a decimetre and a half (6 in.) below the vulva; the wider it is, and the nearer it approaches the vulva, the more milk the cow will give. Above the hinder teats there are two Oval feathers, marked *e, e,* formed of descending hair, and about a decimetre (4 in.) long by five or six centimetres (2.0 or 2.4 in.) wide. To right and left of the vulva are two Buttock feathers of ascending hair, marked *o, o,* which are about four to five centimetres (1.6 to 2 in.) long, and a centimetre (0.4 in.) wide. The hair of these feathers is short, white, and very distinct.

4

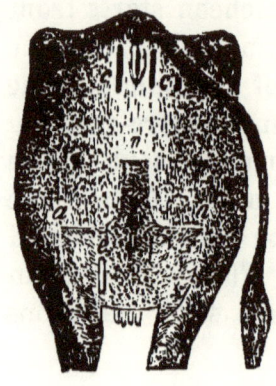

*Second Order.*—Cows of this order give twenty litres (21 quarts) of milk daily, and continue until they are seven months gone with calf. The escutcheon has the same form as in the preceding order, it is only a little less expanded in all its parts. There is but a single Oval feather above the left hinder teat, the feathers to right and left of the vulva are longer than in the preceding order.

*Third Order.*—Cows of this order give sixteen litres (17 quarts) daily, and continue until they are six months gone with calf. The escutcheon is still more contracted than in the preceding order; the points, *a, a,* are nearer together; the line, *n,* is more distant from the vulva. To the right, below the point, *a,* a feather of descending hair, *g,* scoops out a part of the outline. The Buttock feathers are longer and wider than in the preceding order. The left hand one being about twelve cen-

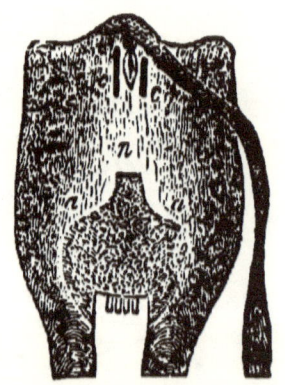

timetres (4.8 in.) in length, by two and a half (1 in.) in width; that on the right is shorter and narrower.

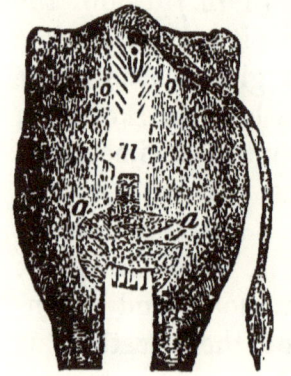

*Fourth Order.*—Cows of this order give twelve litres (12¹/₂ quarts) of milk daily, continuing until they are five months gone with calf. The escutcheon is contracted and lowered. The Buttock feathers to right and left of the vulva are longer and wider; the hair is coarser and more bristling. On the right of the escutcheon is the Thigh feather, *g*.

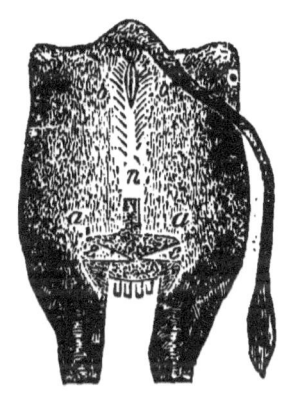

*Fifth Order.*—Cows of this order give nine litres (9$\frac{1}{2}$ quarts) of milk daily, and stop milking when four months gone with calf. The escutcheon is notably reduced in all its proportions. The Buttock and Thigh feathers are longer and wider than in the fourth order.

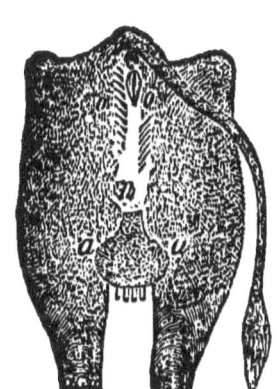

*Sixth Order.*—Cows of this order give six litres (6 quarts) of milk daily, and stop milking when three months gone with calf. The escutcheon is small, and contracted in all its parts. The Buttock feathers are still wider and longer.

### MEDIUM SIZE.

The yield of Demijohn cows of medium size is the same in quantity and persistence as that of Flandrines of the same size and order.

### SMALL SIZE.

Same as for Flandrines of the same size and order.

### BASTARDS.

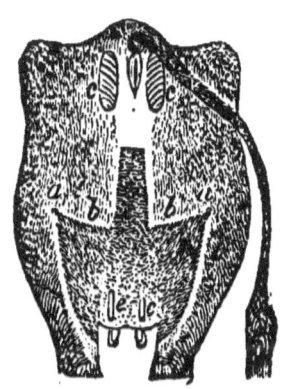

Bastards of this class can be recognized by the Buttock feathers, *c,c*, when these reach the dimensions of

twelve to fifteen centimetres (4.8 to 6 in.) in length
by six or eight (2.4 or 3.2 in.) in width.

### EIGHTH CLASS.—SQUARE COWS.

The name is sufficiently explained by the form of the
escutcheon, which, at the top, is shaped like a carpenter's square.

#### LARGE SIZE.

*First Order.*—Cows of this order give, when in full
milking, twenty-two litres (23 quarts) of milk daily, and

continue until they are eight months gone with calf.
The epidermis of the escutcheon of ascending hair, has
the same color as in the first orders of the preceding
classes, the udder is elastic, and covered with short fine
down. The escutcheon starts from the middle of the
four teats, spreads within over the inner part of the
thighs, stops a little above the houghs, and expands to
the points marked *a, a.* It is there bounded above by two
horizontal lines starting from those points, and re-entering to the points, *j, j,* whence it ascends, as in the Demijohn class, to within five or six centimetres (2 to 2.4

in.) of the vulva, at *o*, from which point a horizontal band turns off to the left at *p*. From the point, *p*, springs a vertical line rising as high as the top of the vulva, at *s*, forming, with the preceding band, the figure of a carpenter's square. Above the hinder teats are two oval feathers marked *e*, as in the first orders of the other classes. Those squares which approach nearest the vulva, and are composed of the finest hair, indicate the best milkers.

*Second Order.*—Cows of this order give eighteen litres (19 quarts) of milk daily, continuing until they are eight months gone with calf. The escutcheon has the same form as in the previous order, but is more contracted in all its parts. The square is further below the vulva, and the ascending fillet consequently longer. There are two Oval feathers, *e, e,* above the hinder teats, and the Buttock feather, *c*, is found on the right of the vulva.

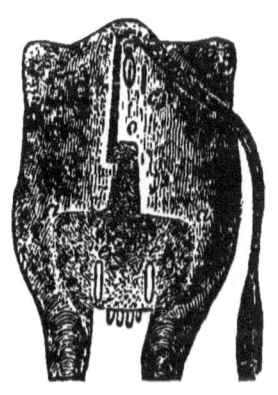

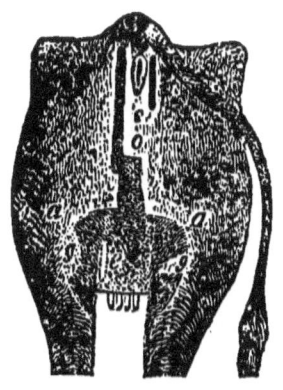

*Third Order.*—Cows of this order give fourteen litres (15 quarts) of milk daily, continuing until they are six months gone with calf. The form of the escutcheon remains the same, but is still more contracted, the square has fallen to three decimetres (12 in.) below the vulva. To the right of the vulva is a feather, *c*, of ascending hair of about eight centimetres (3.2 in.) in length by two and a half (1 in.) in width. On the left, above the teats, is found the Oval feather, marked *e*.

*Fourth Order.*—Cows of this order give ten litres (10¹/₂ quarts) of milk daily, continuing until they are five months gone with calf. The escutcheon has become still smaller; the points, *a, a,* are lowered, and the square has descended. The ascending fillet, on reaching the vulva, is formed of bristling hairs, deviating a little from the vertical as they ascend. The part on the right is also elongated and bristling. The Thigh feather or gore appears at *g.*

*Fifth Order.*—Cows of this order give seven litres (7 quarts) of milk daily, continuing until they are four months gone with calf. The lower part of the escutcheon is greatly contracted, and forms a sort of triangle, truncated and rounded off at the teats. The square is very low, its hair is coarse and bristling, as is that of the feather to the right of the vulva. There are two Thigh feathers or gores at *g, g.*

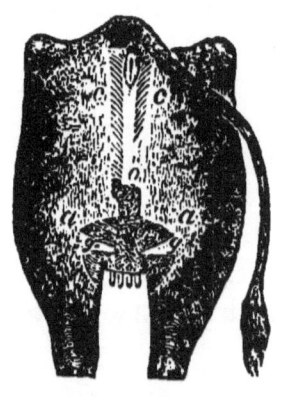

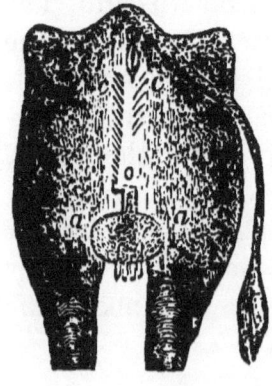

*Sixth Order.*—Cows of this order give four litres (4 quarts) of milk daily, continuing until they are three months gone with calf. The form of the escutcheon is scarcely distinguishable on the animal; the square is down on the thighs. The fillet ascending to the vulva is more bristling and larger than the feather to the right.

## MEDIUM SIZE.

The yield of cows of medium size is the same, as to quantity and persistence, as that of Left-hand Flandrines of the same size and order.

## SMALL SIZE.

Same as for Left-hand Flandrines of the same size and order.

## BASTARDS.

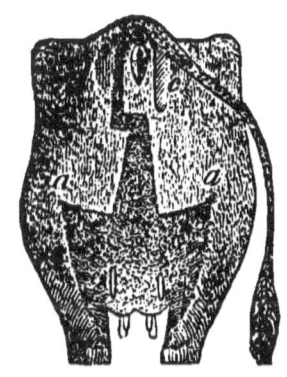

Bastards of Square cows are distinguished by one feature only; the feather, $c$, to the right of the vulva, is of bristling hair. This feature indicates degeneration in all the orders, a degeneration greater or less in proportion to the length and width of the escutcheon and the feather, and greatest when the ascending fillet, to the left of the vulva, is of bristling hair like the feather on the right.

## NINTH CLASS.—LIMOUSINES.

The first cow of this class which came under my observation was of Limoges, and this suggested the name of the class. It must not, however, be supposed that it is confined to cows of that province; it is found in all breeds, with all its orders and their characteristic marks. The escutcheon of Limousine cows assumes the form of a spear-point or arrow-head as it ascends toward the vulva.

*First Order.*—Limousine cows of large size give, when in full milking, twenty litres (21 quarts) of milk daily, continuing until they are eight months gone with calf. The skin of the escutcheon is of the same color as in the preceding classes; the udder is supple, and covered with a soft silky down. The escutcheon starts from the middle of the four teats, extends within and above the houghs, ascending and expanding over the thighs as far as the points, *a, a.* Two transverse lines starting from these

points, re-enter, sloping a little downwards, as far as the points, *j, j,* which are about a decimetre (4 in.) apart. From the points, *j, j,* arise two converging lines, meeting at an acute angle at the point *o,* about a decimetre (4 in.) below the vulva. On the right and left of the vulva are two Buttock feathers, *c, c,* of ascending hair; these are about five centimetres (2 in.) long by about one (0.4 in.) wide. Above the hinder teats are two Oval feathers of descending hair, marked *e, e,* of the same dimensions as those in the preceding classes.

*Second Order.*—Cows of this order give sixteen litres (17 quarts) of milk daily, and continue until they are eight months gone with calf. The escutcheon of this order resembles that of the first, but is more contracted. The lines, *a, j,* are horizontal and more distant from the vulva. The feathers to right and left of the vulva are longer and wider, and there is but a single Oval feather above the teats.

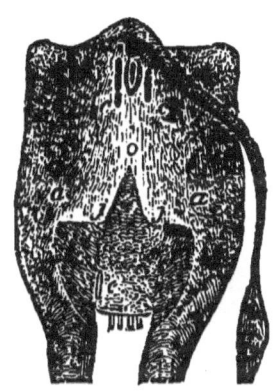

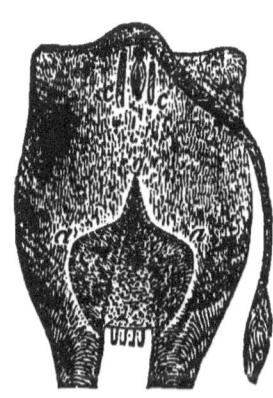

*Third Order.*—Cows of this order give twelve litres (12¹/₂ quarts) of milk daily, continuing until they are six months gone with calf. The escutcheon is still more contracted. The Buttock feather, *c,* of ascending hair, to the left of the vulva, is longer and wider than that on the right, and is of coarser hair. There is no Oval feather above the teats, and the point, *o,* is further removed from the vulva.

*Fourth Order.*—Cows of this order give nine litres (9¹/₂ quarts) of milk daily, and continue until they are five months gone with calf. The escutcheon is narrower and lower. The points, *a, a,* are more depressed, and the whole escutcheon takes rather a rounded form. The point, *o,* is still nearer the teats. The feathers to right and left of the vulva are of bristling hair;

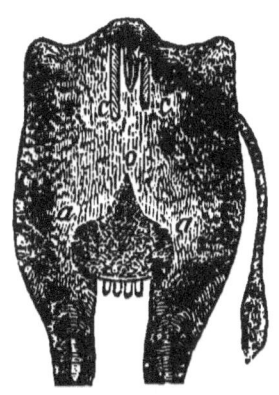

that on the left is fifteen centimetres (6 in.) long and
two (0.8 in.) wide; that on the right is eight centimetres
(3.2 in.) long by two (0.8 in.) wide.

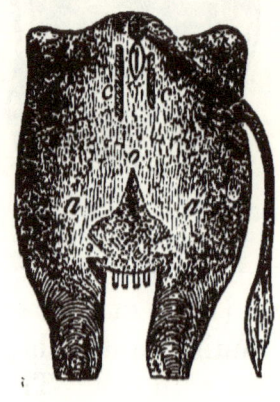

*Fifth Order.*—Cows of this order
give six litres (6 quarts) of milk
daily, and continue until four
months gone with calf. The escutcheon is now quite rounded.
The point, *o*, is distant from the
vulva. Deep between the thighs appear two Thigh feathers, *g*, of descending hair, of greater or less
size, indicating a suppression of
milk. The Buttock feathers on
each side of the vulva are larger than in the preceding
order.

*Sixth Order.*—Cows of this order
give three litres (3 quarts) of milk
daily, and cease milking when
three months gone with calf. The
escutcheon, though similar in form
to the preceding, is withdrawn so
deeply between the thighs as to be
scarcely distinguishable. The Buttock feathers are longer, wider,
and more bristling, a sign of degeneration.

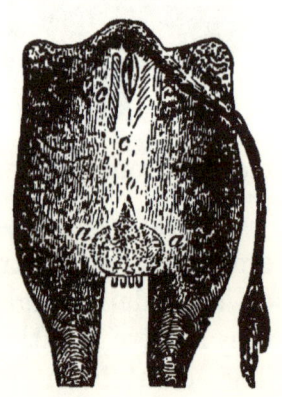

**MEDIUM SIZE.**

*First Order.*—Cows of this order give fifteen litres
(16 quarts) of milk daily, and continue until eight
months gone with calf.

*Second Order.*—Twelve litres (12$\frac{1}{2}$ quarts) daily, until
seven months gone with calf.

*Third Order.*—Nine litres (9¹/₂ quarts) daily, until six months with calf.

*Fourth Order.*—Six litres (6 quarts) daily, until five months with calf.

*Fifth Order.*—Three litres (3 quarts) daily, until four months with calf.

*Sixth Order.*—Two litres (2 quarts) daily, until three months with calf.

### SMALL SIZE.

*First Order.*—Ten litres (10¹/₂ quarts) daily, until eight months with calf.

*Second Order.*—Eight litres (8 quarts) daily, until seven months with calf.

*Third Order.*—Six litres (6 quarts) daily, until six months with calf.

*Fourth Order.*—Four litres (4 quarts) daily, until five months with calf.

*Fifth Order.*—Two litres (2 quarts) daily, until four months with calf.

*Sixth Order.*—One litre (1 quart) daily, until three months with calf.

### BASTARDS.

The feathers of ascending hair to right and left of the vulva, marked *c, c,* have the same length and width as in the bastard Curvelines and Bicorns. They are the characteristic signs of bastard, and degenerate cows in this class.

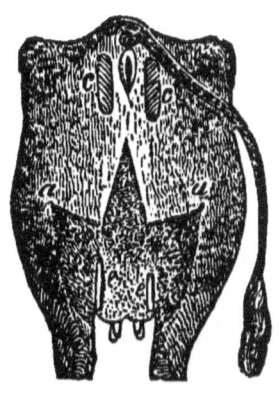

### TENTH CLASS.—CARRESINES.

I have given the name of Carresines to those cows whose escutcheon is terminated above by a horizontal line.

**LARGE SIZE.**

*First Order.*—Cows of this size and order give, when in full milking, twenty litres (21 quarts) of milk daily,

and continue until eight months gone with calf. The escutcheon of this class differs from the others by its flat horizontal top. The pellicles which can be detached from it, resemble a yellow dust; the hair is short, fine, and silky. The escutcheon starts from the middle of the four teats, extends within, and a little above the houghs, spreads upon the thighs as it ascends, to the points *a, a,* where it is bounded by a horizontal line from thigh to thigh, dividing the udder in the middle. Although the escutcheon of this class is farther from the vulva than in any of the others, the cows are none the less good, especially when they have two Buttock feathers, *c, c,* of ascending hair, to right and left of the vulva. These feathers indicate the continuance of milk during pregnancy, they measure from seven to eight centimetres (2.8 to 3.2 in.) in length, by one (0.4 in.) in width. Above the hinder teats are two Oval feathers of descending hair, of a whitish color, and of the same size as in the preceding classes.

*Second Order.*—Cows of this order give sixteen litres (17 quarts) of milk daily, and continue until seven months gone with calf. The es-
cutcheon has the same form, but is more contracted below. The feathers to right and left of the vulva are of unequal size, that to the right being from two to three centimetres (0.8 to 1.2 in.) shorter than the other. There is but one Oval feather, on the left above the hinder teats. Some cows of this class have a Dart feather, five centimetres (2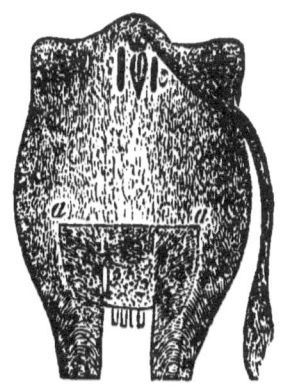
in.) long by one centimetre (0.4 in.) wide, situated immediately beneath the vulva, and terminating below in a point.

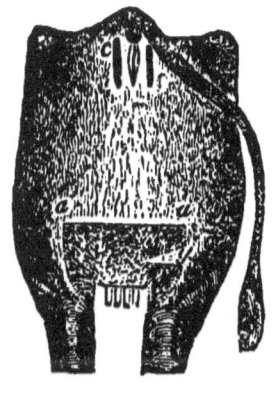

*Third Order.*—Cows of this order give twelve litres (12¹/₂ quarts) of milk daily, and continue until they are six months gone with calf. The escutcheon is more contracted, and lower than in the preceding order. On each side of the vulva is a feather of ascending hair, of eight to ten centimetres (3.2 to 4 in.) in length, by two (0.8 in.) in width. The escutcheon is deeply indented by a notch or gore on one side below the point *a;* it is an

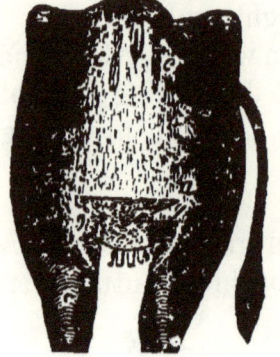

encroachment of descending hair. All the orders of this class are subject to this imperfection.

*Fourth Order.*—Cows of this order give nine litres ($9^1/_2$ quarts) of milk daily, and cease milking when five months gone with calf. The escutcheon has descended still further, and is withdrawn between the thighs. The points, *a, a,* do not extend upon the thighs. The feathers of ascending hair, *c,* to right and left of the vulva, are bristling, and have increased in length and breadth. The Thigh feathers take irregular forms.

*Fifth Order.*—Cows of this order give six litres (6 quarts) of milk daily, continuing until four months gone with calf. The escutcheon is greatly contracted, and the signs of degeneration are still more conspicuous.

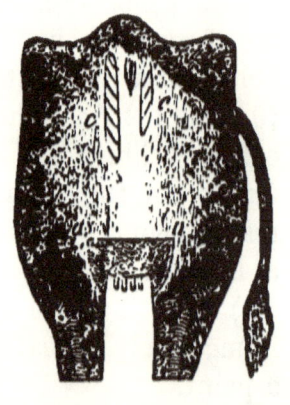

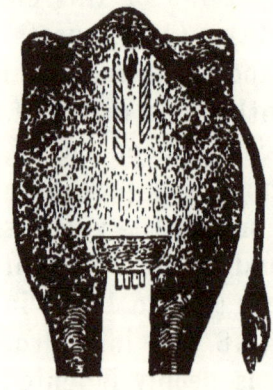

*Sixth Order.*—Cows of this order give three litres (3 quarts) of milk daily, and cease milking when three months gone with calf. The escutcheon is still smaller and very low. The Buttock feathers, *c, c,* are more developed in both length and breadth, and formed of bristling hair; that on the left is always longer than that on the right, and in this case the yield of milk is so diminished as to be insignificant. This degeneration can be yet more considerable, as will be seen by the plates appended to the classification.

### MEDIUM SIZE.

The yield of cows of this size is the same as to quantity and continuance, as with Limousines of the same size and order.

### SMALL SIZE.

The same as with Limousines of the same size and order.

### BASTARDS.

Bastards of this class have the two Buttock feathers of ascending hair, from twelve to fifteen centimetres (4.8 to 6 in.) long. Some of these cows are extremely good milkers when fresh, but they cease milking in a few days after a new impregnation. Those which have a very fine down on the inside of the thighs, give good milk; while the milk of those which have the hair of this part coarse, and transparent, is thin and watery.

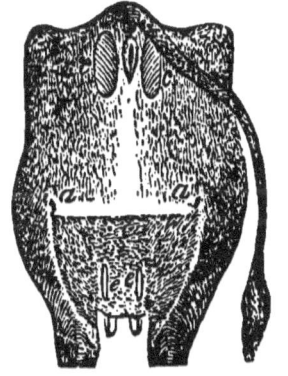

## SYNOPTIC TABLE, EXHIBITING THE YIELD OF MILK OF THE TEN CLASSES OF COWS.

### CONTINUANCE OF MILK DURING PREGNANCY.

| 1st Order. | 2d Order. | 3d Order. | 4th Order. | 5th Order. | 6th Order. |
|---|---|---|---|---|---|
| 8 months. | 7 months. | 6 months. | 5 months. | 4 months. | 3 months. |

### DAILY YIELD OF MILK.

| Nos. of Classes | Classes, or Families. | Size of Animals. | 1st Order. Qts. | 2d Order. Qts. | 3d Order. Qts. | 4th Order. Qts. | 5th Order. Qts. | 6th Order. Qts. |
|---|---|---|---|---|---|---|---|---|
| 1 | Flandrines | Large | 25 | 21 | 17 | 12½ | 9½ | 6 |
|  |  | Medium | 20 | 16 | 12½ | 9½ | 6 | 3 |
|  |  | Small | 15 | 11½ | 8 | 6 | 3 | 1 |
| 2 | Left-Hand Flandrines | Large | 23 | 19 | 15 | 10½ | 7 | 4 |
|  |  | Medium | 18 | 15 | 10½ | 7 | 4 | 2 |
|  |  | Small | 12½ | 10½ | 7 | 4 | 2 | 1 |
| 3 | Selvedge | Large | 25 | 21 | 17 | 12½ | 9½ | 6 |
|  |  | Medium | 20 | 16 | 12½ | 9½ | 6 | 3 |
|  |  | Small | 15 | 11½ | 8 | 6 | 3 | 1 |
| 4 | Curvelines | Large | 25 | 21 | 17 | 12½ | 9½ | 6 |
|  |  | Medium | 20 | 16 | 12½ | 9½ | 6 | 3 |
|  |  | Small | 15 | 11½ | 8 | 6 | 3 | 1 |
| 5 | Bicorns | Large | 25 | 21 | 17 | 12½ | 9½ | 6 |
|  |  | Medium | 20 | 16 | 12½ | 9½ | 6 | 3 |
|  |  | Small | 15 | 11½ | 8 | 6 | 3 | 1 |
| 6 | Double Selvedge | Large | 23 | 19 | 15 | 10½ | 7 | 4 |
|  |  | Medium | 18 | 15 | 10½ | 7 | 4 | 2 |
|  |  | Small | 12½ | 10½ | 7 | 4 | 2 | 1 |
| 7 | Demijohns | Large | 25 | 21 | 17 | 12½ | 9½ | 6 |
|  |  | Medium | 20 | 16 | 12½ | 9½ | 6 | 3 |
|  |  | Small | 15 | 11½ | 8 | 6 | 3 | 1 |
| 8 | Square | Large | 23 | 19 | 15 | 10½ | 7 | 4 |
|  |  | Medium | 18 | 15 | 10½ | 7 | 4 | 2 |
|  |  | Small | 12½ | 10½ | 7 | 4 | 2 | 1 |
| 9 | Limousines | Large | 21 | 17 | 12½ | 9½ | 6 | 3 |
|  |  | Medium | 16 | 12½ | 9½ | 6 | 3 | 2 |
|  |  | Small | 10½ | 8 | 6 | 4 | 2 | 1 |
| 10 | Carresines | Large | 21 | 17 | 12½ | 9½ | 6 | 3 |
|  |  | Medium | 16 | 12½ | 9½ | 6 | 3 | 2 |
|  |  | Small | 10½ | 8 | 6 | 4 | 2 | 1 |

REMARK.—Bastard Cows of all the classes and orders only differ from "free" cows in losing their milk almost immediately after a new impregnation.

ESCUTCHEONS OMITTED IN THE CLASSIFICATION,
FORMING THE SEVENTH AND EIGHTH ORDERS
OF EACH CLASS.

FIRST CLASS.—FLANDRINES.

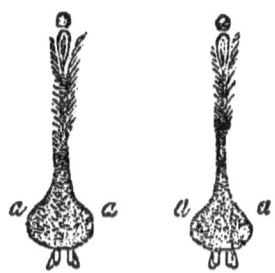

*Seventh and Eighth Orders.*

SECOND CLASS.—LEFT-HAND FLANDRINES.

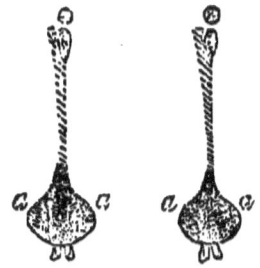

*Seventh and Eighth Orders*

THIRD CLASS.—SELVEDGE.

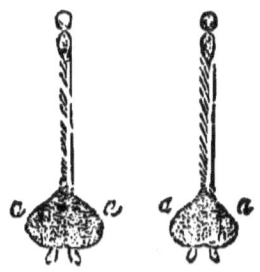

*Seventh and Eighth Orders.*

## FOURTH CLASS.—CURVELINES.

*Seventh and Eighth Orders.*

## FIFTH CLASS.—BICORNS.

*Seventh and Eighth Orders.*

## SIXTH CLASS.—DOUBLE SELVEDGE.

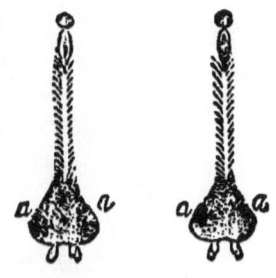

*Seventh and Eighth Orders.*

SEVENTH CLASS.—DEMIJOHNS.

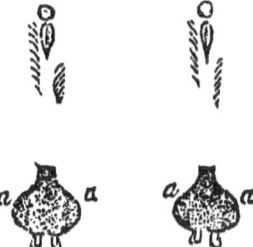

*Seventh and Eighth Orders.*

EIGHTH CLASS.—SQUARE COWS.

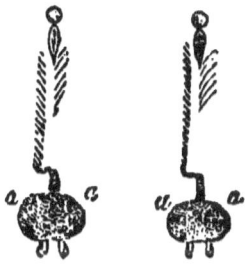

*Seventh and Eighth Orders.*

NINTH CLASS.—LIMOUSINES.

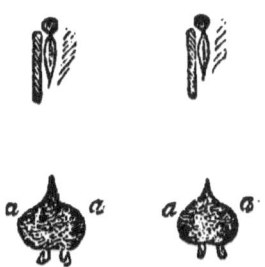

*Seventh and Eighth Orders.*

TENTH CLASS.—CARRESINES.

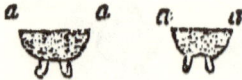

*Seventh and Eighth Orders.*

These supplementary orders being of rather rare occurrence, I have figured them here as an appendix to
the classification.

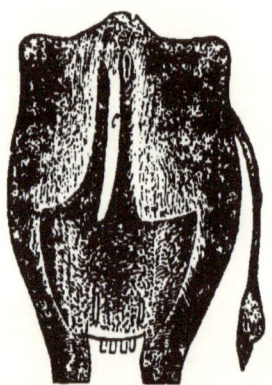

NEW ESCUTCHEONS REFERRED
TO IN THE INTRODUCTION.

CROSS OF SELVEDGE AND LEFT-
HAND FLANDRINE.

Cows of this description are tol-
erably common in certain breeds,
and especially those of the north-
east of France.

CROSS OF BICORN AND SELVEDGE.

The Dart feather, as I call it,
which may be seen at *n*, adhering
to the vulva, is a favorable indication, and may occur in any of those
classes in which the escutcheon does
not reach the vulva. Cows which
have either of the escutcheons last
given are usually good milkers, and
preserve their milk like those of
the first orders of each class.

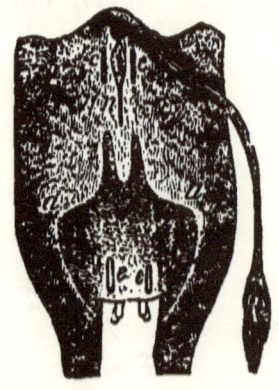

# CHAPTER VI.

## BULLS AND THEIR CLASSIFICATION.

### OF BULLS IN GENERAL.

Having described in the preceding chapter the various
orders of cows, and explained the manner of distinguishing the bastards of each class, I pass to the distinctive
signs found in bulls, which also may be divided into
classes and orders. The signs are similar to those of
cows, but much more contracted, that is, the surface ex-
hibiting them is smaller. In bulls, the escutcheon starts
just above, and within the houghs, spreads over the
hinder surface of the thighs, and in the higher orders of
certain classes, ascends as high as the anus. As with
cows, the escutcheons of bulls are modified by the presence
of feathers. Those bulls whose escutcheons, in form and
dimensions, resemble those of cows of the higher orders,
are well adapted to the procreation of offspring of good
milking qualities; while those, on the contrary, whose
escutcheon is but little developed, will only produce degenerate offspring.

A bull is well marked, and shows the indications of a
good calf-getter, when there is no invasion of descending
hair into the ascending hair of his escutcheon; when the
escutcheon is of large dimensions, in proportion to the

(93)

size of the animal, and is covered with very fine hair. Those which have small escutcheons covered with hair that flares off toward the sides, will beget offspring of bad milking qualities, and yielding poor and watery milk. Every invasion of the escutcheon by descending hair, on the right, left, and inner surface of the thighs, foretells bastardy and degeneration of milking qualities of the off-spring. A yellowish or nankeen color of the skin of the escutcheon, is a favorable indication. A bull of good procreative qualities may occasionally retain his fertility until from ten to fifteen years of age, but these cases are rare exceptions. It is a great mistake to judge the pro-creative powers of a bull by the form, build, and general appearance; experience, or scientifically directed observa-tions alone, can inform us on this point. A bull of good age and condition is able to serve several cows daily, but it is important that he should not be admitted to the fe-male until he has reached the age of fifteen to eighteen months. If he be used too soon, he will exhaust his vigor, and impair his form; his growth and development will be checked. In many provinces the bulls are allowed to serve cows for a period of only twelve or fifteen months; this is especially the case with those animals that are intended for labor or slaughter.

When the bull has reached the age of from eighteen months to three years, his figure changes, his hind-quarters become relatively narrower, while his fore-quarters are greatly developed, his neck grows thick and massive, etc. If at this period he is castrated, whether by removing the testicles, or cutting the spermatic cords (*bistournage,*) he retains this form, and is less fit for work, and less desirable for butchering. Moreover, when castration is deferred too long, the animal has less ten-dency to fatten, his meat is tough and leathery, although in external appearance, in age, and in feeding, he should differ in no respect from animals castrated earlier.

It often happens that bulls of quiet and gentle disposition become fierce and wild after being admitted to the cows. In some provinces a ring of iron, passed through the septum of the nose, is used to control these refractory animals; but where the use of this expedient is not known, castration is the only resource, and if it fails, they must be handed over to the butcher.

## CLASSIFICATION OF BULLS.

Bulls, like cows, may be ranged in ten classes or families, of which each class comprises several orders, and every order three sizes: large, medium, and small. I shall, however, only distinguish three orders in each class, which I shall designate as Good, Fair, and Bad. If it were desired to carry the subdivision closer, the same distinctions could be observed as in cows. The signs which in a bull indicate the property of procreating offspring of good milking qualities, are situated in the same region as the signs of the females. The escutcheon starts from the fore-part of the scrotum, extends within and above the houghs, and spreads out upon the thighs, from which point lines, curved, straight, or angular, according to the class, ascend, and meet below the anus.

The escutcheon, throughout its whole extent, should be marked by fineness of skin and hair, and by a more or less yellow tint of the epidermis and the pellicles, which may be detached from it.

The secondary signs on cows are also found on the bulls. Bulls have four, and sometimes six, small rudimentary teats, situated in front of the scrotum. On the right and left sides of the belly may be seen two veins analogous to the milk-veins of cows, which, starting from the scrotum, extend a little further forward than the navel, and end in a small cavity.

Besides the characteristic signs referred to above, a bull for procreation should unite all those qualities which together constitute the pure type of the breed to which he belongs. These are:—

1.—The color preferred in the breed.

2.—Size proportioned to the breed, and the regular and typical form and build well established.

3.—To be of the first order of the class to which he belongs, that he may transmit the best milking qualities to his progeny.

4.—Tendency to fatten.

5.—Suitability for work.

6.—A gentle and docile disposition.

Defects of organization, like good qualities, are hereditary, and unless this cardinal fact be borne in mind, all attempts to improve a breed will be fruitless.

Down to the present time too little care and attention have been given to the selection of bulls for reproduction, and the result has been a lamentable degeneration, which should be arrested as promptly as possible. To this end I earnestly invite the attention of the administration, both general and local, to a system capable of rendering so important a service to the country as an increased production of the best animals for the pail and for the butcher.

In all breeds, the greater number of bulls will be found to belong to the following classes, arranged in order of frequency:— 1. Curvelines. 2. Limousines. 3. Carresines.

The classes which will be found to have but few representatives, are the following:- 4. Demijohns. 5. Bicorns. 6. Square. 7. Selvedge. 8. Left-hand Flandrines. 9. Double Selvedge. 10. Flandrines.

To explain the reason why bulls of the best reproductive qualities, and belonging to the higher orders of their respective classes, are so rare, we must consider, first, their small number as compared with cows, and, secondly, the impossibility which has hitherto existed of recognizing what calves should be saved for the purposes of reproduction. For want of this knowledge the best animals have been, and still are, sent to the butcher, or castrated when young; and, most frequently, those which have been saved for propagation were those least fitted for the purpose.

For—and this should be noted—animals of the higher orders possess, at the very birth, those qualities which confer superiority : they are easily reared, and, as the mother has abundance of milk, they soon fatten, and are selected for the butcher; while, on the other hand, calves of lower orders, not fattening well, are not so saleable, and so are allowed to become propagators. From such an unnatural selection and survival of the unfittest, nothing but degeneration can be expected.

The first thing, therefore, to be done to improve our breeds, is to amend this practice, and to learn to select, at the earliest age, those animals which will transmit good qualities to their offspring.

## FIRST CLASS.—FLANDRINE BULLS.

These bulls have the escutcheon of the same form as that borne by that class of cows which I have called Flandrines. I place them at the head of the list because they are best fitted to transmit good milking qualities to their progeny; but I must say that they are extremely rare, both in French and foreign breeds ; and in all the districts which I have visited, I have seen but very few.

As I have said, I divide each class into three orders, Good, Fair, and Bad. I also distinguish three sizes:— Large animals, by which I mean those which, at full development, will yield five hundred kilogrammes (1,100 lbs.) of clear meat, on an average. Medium, or those

5

which, under the same conditions, will yield four hundred kilogrammes (880 lbs.). And small, those which will yield from two hundred to two hundred and fifty kilogrammes (440 to 550 lbs).

I make no distinction between these sizes in my description of the escutcheons, and I limit my descriptions to the three principal orders of each class, leaving it to experts, if they choose, to determine the degrees intermediate between Good and Fair, and Fair and Bad.

### FIRST ORDER.—GOOD.

Bulls of this class and order may be recognized by the escutcheon of similar pattern to that of cows of the same

order and class. It is merely less extended in all its parts, for the reason that the tissues which inclose the generative organs in the bull are less developed than those enveloping the milk-giving apparatus of the cow. The feathers of ascending hair, forming the design, start from the lower part of the scrotum, expand to left and right as they ascend within and above the houghs, spread out

on either side, about midway of the buttocks, to the points
*a, a,* where the outline makes two re-entering angles, and
from the middle two lines arise, terminating at the anus
with a breadth of from two to three centimetres (0.8 to
1.2 in.) each.

The skin covering the scrotum should be supple, fine,
and covered with a short and silky or cottony hair, rather
sparse than thick.  The color should be of a shaded,
velvety, yellowish tint, such as I have described when
speaking of cows.  The fine pellicles which may be detached from it, should be unctuous to the touch.  In a
word, in these bulls should be found all the characteristics
of the higher orders of cows, as these characteristics in
the male indicate the transmission of good milking qualities to his progeny.

### SECOND ORDER.—FAIR.

The escutcheon is less developed and less extended in
all its parts : the points, *a, a,* are lower and nearer

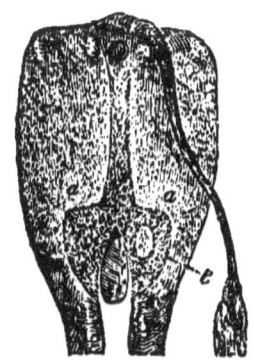

together ; the ascending band is narrower, with bristling hair, especially
on the right side; only on the left
does it rise as high as the anus.  On
the inside of the thigh, about the
middle of the escutcheon, to the
right, will be observed an Oval
feather, *e,* of descending hair, from
three to four centimetres (1.2 to 1.6
in.) wide, by from five to six (2 to
2.4 in.) long.  This denotes inferior-
ity in the progeny, especially when this feather is large,
and covered with long, thick hair.

As a general rule, in all the classes and orders, when this
feather is found not merely on one thigh, but on both,
the animal should be ranked one or more orders lower,

according to the size of the feather.   For the dimensions
of the escutcheon, the second order of bulls may be compared with the third or fourth order of cows of the same
class.

### THIRD ORDER.—BAD.

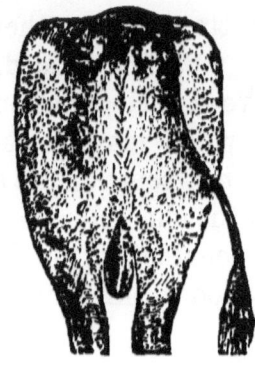

The escutcheon is greatly contracted: it is limited to the lower
part of the thighs, and ascends very
little upon the scrotum, a few bristling hairs alone indicate its presence.
The third order of bulls may be compared, with reference to the size of
the escutcheon, with the sixth order
of cows.

### SECOND CLASS.—LEFT-HAND FLANDRINE BULLS.

Although rare, these are found more frequently in all
breeds than those of the preceding class.

### FIRST ORDER.—GOOD.

Bulls of this order and class have all the characteristics
of cows of the first order of the second class.

The escutcheon of ascending hair starts from above the
inner surface of the houghs, spreading as it ascends, as
far as the middle of the thigh, where it forms angles at
the points *a, a.*   It there re-enters upon the inner surface
of the thighs, and narrows to a vertical band which
ascends on the left buttock as high as the anus, and ends
with a breadth of from three to four centimetres (1.2 to
1.6 in.)   On the right side a horizontal line starts from
the point *a,* runs to the juncture of the thighs, where it

joins the vertical stripe, and terminates at the middle of the anus.   All the characteristics of the hair and skin

should be the same as those of the first order and first class.

### SECOND ORDER.—FAIR.

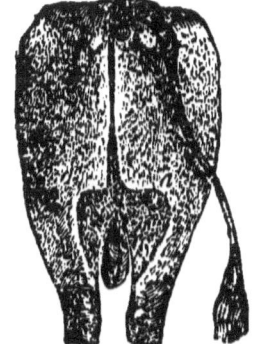

The escutcheon is less developed and smaller than that of the first order: the angles, *a, a,* are lower, and rounded off.  The line of ascending hair on the left thigh disappears when about half-way to the anus.

### THIRD ORDER.—BAD.

The escutcheon, greatly contracted, merely forms an oval inclosing the scrotum a few centimetres above the testicles; from its upper part starts a line of bristling hair, very imperfectly traced, which narrows as it ascends toward the left side of the anus, where it is no longer visible.

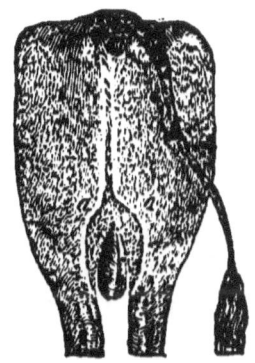

## THIRD CLASS.—SELVEDGE BULLS.

Though by no means numerous, these bulls are more frequently met with than those of the two preceding classes.

### FIRST ORDER.—GOOD.

The escutcheon has the same form as that of cows of the second class and order; it starts from the lower part

of the scrotum, spreads to each side within the thighs, and ascends, widening, to the points *a, a*. From these points start two re-entering lines running toward the juncture of the thighs to within ten centimetres (4 in.) of the median line, whence start two lines of ascending hair converging to the anus and forming a fillet which at its termination has a breadth of from one to two centimetres (0.4 to 0.8 in.).

The character of hair and skin should be the same as in the preceding classes.

### SECOND ORDER.—FAIR.

The escutcheon is narrow and less developed; the points *a, a,* are lowered and rounded. The fillet narrows as it approaches the anus,

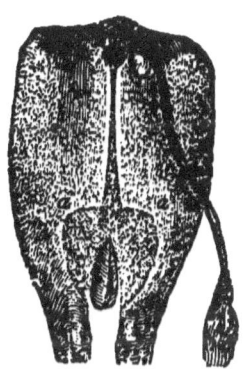

and is more slender than in the preceding order.

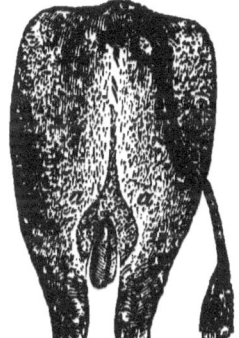

### THIRD ORDER.—BAD.

The escutcheon is still more depressed, and terminates above in a thin, broken line, which ends several centimetres below the anus.

### FOURTH CLASS.—CURVELINE BULLS.

To this class most bulls in all breeds will be found to belong.

### FIRST ORDER.—GOOD.

The form of the escutcheon is the same as that of cows

of the same class ; the larger its extent, the greater the aptitude of the animal to transmit good milking qualities to his progeny. The fineness of the ascending hair, suppleness of the skin, and yellower color, all indicate superiority.

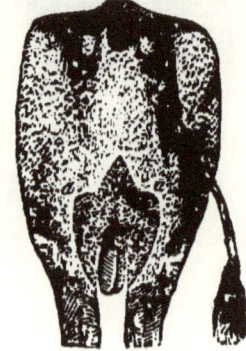

### SECOND ORDER.—FAIR.

The escutcheon is more contracted in all its dimensions, and is more withdrawn within in the thighs. The points, *a, a,* are rounded and lowered.

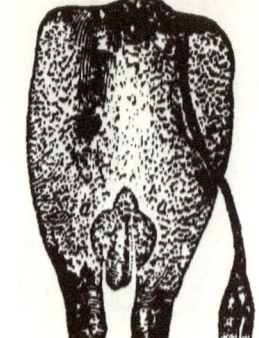

### THIRD ORDER.—BAD.

The escutcheon is now shrunk to the space immediately inclosing the scrotum.

### FIFTH CLASS.—BICORN BULLS.

Bulls of this class are not often met with. When they unite all the characteristics of cows of the first order of the class, they are well adapted to produce offspring of good milking qualities.

### FIRST ORDER.—GOOD.

Escutcheon the same in pattern as that of cows of the

first order of the class. Its upper margin is prolonged into two points or horns of ten to twelve centimetres (4 to 4.8 in.) in length, by about two (0.8 in.) in width; that on the left is the longer. The nearer these horns approach the anus, and the greater the spread of the lower part of the escutcheon upon the thighs, the better will be the progeny.

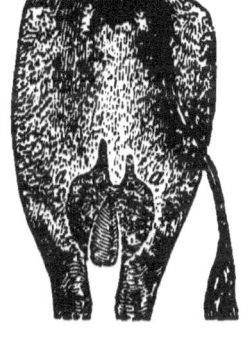

### SECOND ORDER.—FAIR.

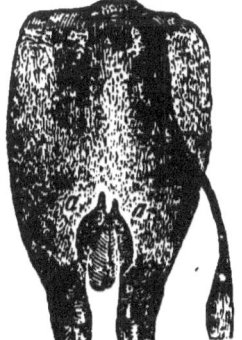

Escutcheon lower and more contracted in all its parts; left horn higher than the right.

### THIRD ORDER.—BAD.

Escutcheon quite shrunken. The two horns are scarcely distinguishable, having drawn nearer together, and sunk almost to the scrotum.

### SIXTH CLASS.—DOUBLE SELVEDGE BULLS.

Bulls of this class are almost as scarce, in all breeds, as the Flandrines, and it would be well to take some pains to look for and preserve them, with a view to the improvement of the stock.

#### FIRST ORDER.—GOOD.

The escutcheon of this class appears at first glance very closely to resemble that of the Flandrines. It is divided into two equal parts by a band of downward-growing hair, which, starting from the anus, descends vertically to the testicles. The more sharply marked this division, and

the finer the texture and color of the hair and skin, the better the animal.

### SECOND ORDER.—FAIR.

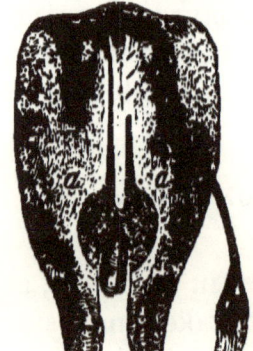

The lower part of the escutcheon is rounded and depressed; the left-hand fillet alone ascends to the anus, while that on the right stops mid-way. Both fillets are nearer the median line than in the preceding order.

### THIRD ORDER.—BAD.

Escutcheon still more depressed, and the fillets narrower and closer than in the preceding order. That on the right ends at about two-thirds the distance from the anus, and that on the left at about one-third. They are, however, in some sort continued by a few bristling hairs.

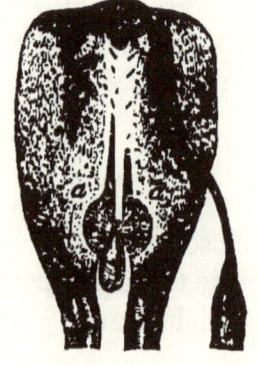

### SEVENTH CLASS.—DEMIJOHN BULLS.

Bulls of this class are rather scarce, but are more frequently met with than those of the preceding.

#### FIRST ORDER.—GOOD.

The escutcheon is identical with that of cows of the same class and order ; the down which clothes it and the

perinæum above as high as the anus, is fine, silky, and velvety. The color of the epidermis is yellowish, as is that of the unctuous dust which may be detached from it.

Bulls of this order, combining in a high degree the characteristics above mentioned, are well adapted to transmit good milking qualities.

#### SECOND ORDER.—FAIR.

The escutcheon, depressed in all its parts, presents the form of a small obese jar or demijohn.

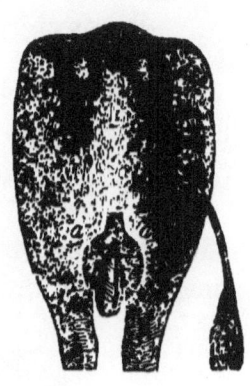

### THIRD ORDER.—BAD.

Escutcheon still more depressed, and greatly shrunken. Its form is usually irregular.

### EIGHTH CLASS.—SQUARE BULLS.

These are still rarer in all breeds than the Bicorns and Demijohns; they are met with, however, now and then, and those of the first order are good propagators.

### FIRST ORDER.—GOOD.

The form of the escutcheon is the same in its lower part as that of the Selvedge class; but the band of ascend-

ing hair is interrupted about six or eight centimetres (2.4 or 3.2 in.) below the anus, and takes the form of a square, or bayonet turned to the left, on which side it rises as high as the anus.    In other respects, the marks are the same as those of cows of the same class and order.

### SECOND    ORDER.—FAIR.

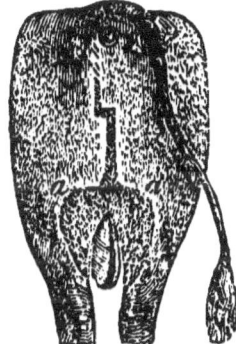

The base of the escutcheon is rounded and depressed, as in the same order of other classes. The line which turns to the left to form the square, starts at about fifteen centimetres (6 in.) below the anus, and the point rising like a bayonet, is broken at the upper part.

### THIRD    ORDER.—BAD.

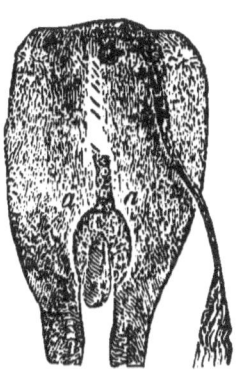

Escutcheon still more contracted and depressed; the square scarcely perceptible, and the rising point becomes a broken line of bristles.

### NINTH    CLASS.—LIMOUSINE BULLS.

These are of frequent occurrence in all races.    They can only be considered good when the escutcheon is well developed, and presents the characteristics of the first order.

### FIRST    ORDER.—GOOD.

Form of the escutcheon the same as with cows of the first order of the class.    The spear-shaped ascending point should reach within about a decimetre (4 in.) of the anus, and be formed of short, fine, and silky hair.   The

skin should have the fineness, color, and unctuous feel of
the first orders.

### SECOND ORDER.—FAIR.

Escutcheon contracted; the angles
lower and rounded off; the spear-
shaped point is smaller, and more
distant from the anus.

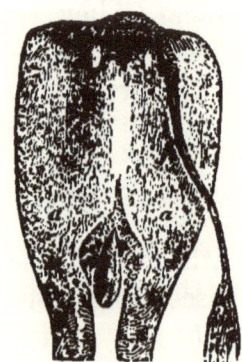

### THIRD ORDER.—BAD.

Escutcheon still more depressed,
and shrunken in all its parts; it
barely incloses the scrotum.

## TENTH CLASS.—CARRESINE BULLS.

These bulls are numerous in all breeds; they are only good when the escutcheon has all the characteristics of that of cows of the first order of this class.

### FIRST ORDER.—GOOD.

The escutcheon starts from the testicles, and rises to about a decimetre (4 in.) above the scrotum; a transverse

line bounds it at the top, reaching to the points *a, a,* on the thighs. As in the other classes, the hair ascends within and above the houghs, and spreads upon the thighs to the points *a, a.* Bulls of the first order should have the inner surface and juncture of the thighs of a yellowish color, as in cows of the first order of the same class.

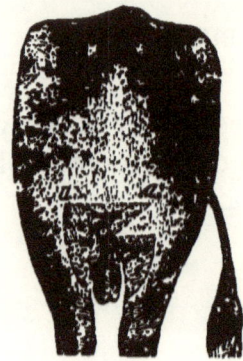

### SECOND ORDER.—FAIR.

The escutcheon preserves the same form and color, but is smaller. Under the point *a*, on the right side, is found the thigh feather.

### THIRD ORDER.—BAD.

Escutcheon still more contracted; it only covers the surface of the scrotum, which it seems to separate from the surface above, by a horizontal line.

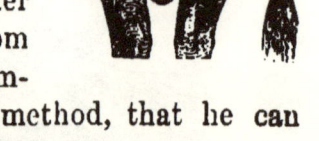

I close this chapter, which completes my general classification, with one earnest request to the reader who is seriously interested in the subject, to neglect none of the details which it contains; it is only after having followed up my work from point to point, and familiarized himself with the application of my method, that he can become a thoroughly qualified judge.

# BOOK II.

## CHAPTER I.

### THE FOUR CONDITIONS WHICH ANIMALS OF EITHER SEX SHOULD UNITE TO FORM THE PERFECT TYPE.

1.—Handsome build and regular proportions.

2.—Escutcheon of the first order of its class.

3.—Aptitude for fattening.

4.—Gentleness of disposition.

The combination of these qualities forms the perfect type.

# CHAPTER II.

## OF HANDSOME AND UGLY TYPES.

### HANDSOME TYPES.

That attraction which beauty of form exercises upon us, at the first glance, is a thing which no one can contemn; yet abundant experience has shown that in many respects the goodness of an animal is independent of its beauty. On the other hand, it is true that extreme ugliness borders very closely on certain defects of conformation, the transmission of which to the progeny is to be feared, and should be avoided if possible.

In certain localities, preference is given to particular forms, colors, configuration of head or horns, etc., and types which unite these peculiarities, are those which breeders aim at perpetuating. But, as I have said before, the perfection and extent of the milk escutcheon, the development of the *manets* (described hereafter), the muscular strength, or fitness for work, and docility of disposition, should be more regarded than mere beauty of form.

Still there is a type of bovine beauty which all judges recognize. All agree in admiring those animals, of either sex, which have a straight back, wide shoulders and loins, haunches not too prominent, slender bones, round sides, short and full neck, narrow flanks. Tail thick at its root, and thin near the switch, well set on, neither too high nor too low. Houghs flat, broad, a little arched backwards. Buttocks round, thigh well thickened down toward the hough. Fore-legs well set apart, and very slightly bent inwards (knock-kneed). Chest wide and deep, well carried forward, and developed at the curve about twenty centi-

(114)

metres (8 in.) from the knee. Dewlap of medium size, and handsome shape. Head short and square. Eyes large and prominent. Nostrils wide. Muzzle fine and slightly turned up (*camard*). Lips small and regular. Ear furry, with long hairs in the interior (a sign of strength and energy)—finally, an unctuous epidermis. Horns fine, and of medium length, and the tuft between the horns not very long-haired.

## UGLY TYPES.

Those animals are displeasing to the eye, which have protuberences on the back, flat sides, long flanks, thin thighs. The croupe swollen out, or hollowed out. Head long or too stumpy, pointed muzzle. Horns disproportionately large, and long. Projecting bones. Narrow chest. Too much dewlap or none. Hind-legs too much bent or too straight. Hoofs flattened out as if crushed by the heavy and clumsy tread. It is true that an individual may have these deformities, and yet possess valuable qualities; but in breeding these types should be shunned, as the progeny will be degenerate.

## CONCLUSION.

In breeding we should select animals of the handsomest type. In young animals we look for slender legs, round feet, hoofs and false hoofs (*onglons*) short, which predict a great development in size. Thin and flexible skin, fine hair, bristling a little, or cottony, silky, or curly, are indications of good health, and a gentle, docile disposition. To facilitate the student in his examinations, I here subjoin a synopsis of the physical characteristics or points, which should be found in animals of either sex of the finest types, and belonging to the first orders of their respective classes. The order followed, is that usually observed in the examination of the animal.

## POINTS OF THE HANDSOME TYPE.

1.—Skin of the color most esteemed in the particular breed.

2.—Size proportionate.

3.—Escutcheon of the first order.

4.—Epidermis of escutcheon fine and yellowish.

5.—Udder round, well shaped, and teats regular.

6.—Spine straight and level.

7.—Bones slender.

8.—The whole hide thin and flexible.

9.—Loins wide.

10.—Haunches not too prominent.

11.—Tail well set on, thick at the root, and slender at the switch.

12.—Croupe neither too high nor too low.

13.—Buttocks round.

14.—Thighs low and muscular.

15.—Sides round.

16.—Flanks narrow.

17.—Shoulders wide.

18.—Dewlap of medium size.

19.—Chest large, deep, and well rounded.

20.—Neck short and of medium thickness.

21.—Head short and square.

22.—Ears of medium size and hairy within.

23.—Eyes large and prominent.

24.—Horns medium.

25.—Tuft between the horns not too hairy.

26.—Nostrils wide.

27.—Muzzle short and a little turned up.

28.—Lips rather thin.

29.—Houghs flat, wide, not too much arched backward.

30.—Legs fine and straight.

31.—False hoofs short.

32.—Feet round.

# CHAPTER III.

## THE "MANETS," OR FATTY LUMPS.

SUMMARY.—Description of the Manets.—The shoulder-vein.—The forethigh.—The fore-udder.—The mid-buttock.—The scrotum.—The -pelvic margin.—The collar-vein.—The chest.—The rib.—The flank.—The loin.—The haunch.—The neck-vein.—The carlet.— The under-jaw—General remarks.

### THE MANETS.

These are agglomerations of fat, of various forms, embedded in the subcutaneous cellular tissue. They may be soft or hard, fixed or movable. Each has a certain signification of value in estimating the aptitude of an animal for fattening, and its existing condition of fat. Although animals bred under similar circumstances may present, at a first inspection, no differences of form, yet an examination of these manets may point out to us great differences, or enable us to rectify an erroneous judgment. An animal may be lean and bony, and yet be well adapted for fattening, while another has a fleshy appearance, and yet is of poor quality when slaughtered. As a general rule, the primitive races which have furnished the original types of each class, have an aptitude for fattening; nevertheless we meet in all breeds animals which are exceptionally well or ill fitted to take on fat. The germ of the tendency to fatten exists in the cellular tissues, which lie between the skin and the flesh, and extend inwardly into the less muscular parts of the animal. In these tissues are formed lumps, or agglomerations of fat, technically called "manets." They are of

(117)

various forms and thicknesses, some round, others flat or elongated, and they vary in thickness according to the greater or less fatness of the animal, and its greater or less tendency to take on fat.

Those animals which will yield tender, fat, and juicy meat, have a thin skin, and dappled, fine, and short hair. The flesh below shows through the delicate skin, and sometimes presents as appetizing an appearance as a freshly gathered peach. Those, on the contrary, whose tissues do not form fat, have a dry, hard, and thick skin; their meat is dry, tough, and less nutritious. The presence of the manets, however small they may be, is a test of the superiority of the animal, and they may easily be detected under the skin, by compressing it with the tips of the fingers. As they develop in proportion to the increase of fat, it is easy to determine by comparison those animals which will fatten most readily. As an example, I will suppose an individual of medium fatness, and the manet to be examined, to be that which I call the shoulder-vein.

This can be detected as soon as it is formed; even when no thicker than a bit of twine, it can be felt to roll between the skin and the flesh; and will perceptibly grow as the animal fattens. When it has reached the thickness of the little finger, we may be sure that the flesh is of good quality; if it enlarges still further, to the thickness of the thumb, or thicker, the improvement is still greater, and the meat will be, both as to quantity and quality, all that can be desired.

DESCRIPTION OF THE MANETS.

The entire number of these manets is fifteen, viz.:

1.—The Shoulder-vein Manet.
2.—The Fore-Thigh Manet.
3.—The Fore-Udder Manet.
4.—The Mid-Buttock Manet.
5.—The Scrotum Manet.
6.—The Pelvic Basin Manet.
7.—The Collar-vein Manet.
8.—The Chest Manet.
9.—The Side Manet.
10.—The Flank Manet.
11.—The Loin Manet.
12.—The Haunch Manet.
13.—The Neck-vein Manet.
14.—The Earlet Manet.
15.—The Under-Jaw Manet.

The most important of these on the cow are Nos. 1, 2, 3, 4, and 6. On the bullock, Nos. 1, 2, 5, and 6. Upon these we chiefly found our judgment, the others have but a secondary value in confirming their indications.

### 1.—THE SHOULDER-VEIN.

This is found upon the shoulder-blade, near its upper posterior margin, and descends vertically as far as the joint of the leg. It is flexible, rather long than round, and can be felt by pressing with the fingers. That on the left is usually longer than the other. (In comparing animals, the same sides should be examined.) On steers or cows of the first quality, it seems to the touch to have a thickness of about five centimetres (2 in.), of three (1.2 in.) on those of second quality, and one (0.4 in.) on the third. On lean animals it is not easily distinguished.

### 2.—THE FORE-THIGH.

This is flexible to the touch, and is found on both sides, that on the right being the larger. It is situated on the fore-part of the thigh, in the fold of skin that joins the belly, and extends upon the belly at the lower part of the flank. It is rather flat than round. In a fat animal it can be distinctly seen in walking. When the leg is brought forward, it rises under the skin like a ball ; but the thickness can best be determined by grasping it. The fatness of the animal will always be in proportion to its thickness. In large animals in fine condition it has three decimetres (12 in.) in length, two (8 in.) in width, and one (4 in.) in thickness. In animals of second and third quality, it will have two-thirds and one-third of these dimensions.

### 3.—THE FORE-UDDER.

This is only found upon cows : it is situated on the belly, between the navel and the udder, to which it adheres. It is flexible, flat, and rounded a little in the middle. Its size, for the first quality, is two to three decimetres (8 to 12 in.) long, by two and one-half (10 in.) wide, and one (4 in.) thick. In animals of second and third quality, it is one-third and two-thirds smaller.

### 4.—THE MID-BUTTOCK.

This also is peculiar to females : it is situated at the juncture of the thighs, between the buttocks, and rises vertically to the vulva. Its form is that of a cord, and it is flexible when the animal is about half-fattened. On a fat cow it is firm and hard, and if compressed transversely, gives a thickness of from seven to eight centimetres (2.8 to 3.2 in.) for the first quality, four to five (1.6 to 2 in.) for the second, and one to two (0.4 to 0.8 in.) for the third.

### 5.—THE SCROTUM.

This is the manet which should first be looked for in the examination of bullocks.

Those animals which have had the spermatic cords cut (*le bistournage*), have testicles about the size of a walnut, embedded in a mass of fat, which is full, hard, and firm in beeves of the first quality. Those in which the scrotum hangs low, approaching near the houghs, are preferred. Animals castrated by removal of the testicles, have the juncture of the thighs placed higher up. With them this manet is neither so large nor so low, and to determine 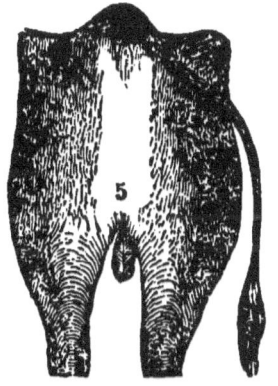 its volume, it must be grasped in the hand. The quality of the animal will be in proportion to its size and firmness.

### 6.—THE PELVIC MARGIN.

This occupies the space on each side of the root of the tail; it is rather flat than round, and must be felt to be estimated. In animals of the first quality it has a thickness of a decimeter (4 in.), in the second, six centimetres (2.4 in.), and in the third, two to three centimetres (0.8 to 1.2 in.). It indicates the quantity of subcutaneous fat.

6

### 7.—THE COLLAR-VEIN.

This is flexible and rolling; it is situated at the upper front margin of the shoulder, and forms a kind of round vein, in a vertical position, of from two to three decimetres (8 to 12 in.) in length. It is judged by compressing it crosswise in the middle, and for the first quality should have a thickness of from four to five centimetres (1.6 to 2 in.), for the second, a third less, and for the third quality, two-thirds less. It indicates the quantity of internal fat.

### 8.—THE CHEST.

This is found on the bony part of the sternum or brisket, in front, between the forelegs. It is always formed of firm fat, and indicates the general plumpness of the animal. The thickness for the first quality is from twelve to fifteen centimetres (4.8 to 6 in.), for the second, from eight to nine (3.2 to 3.6 in.), and for the third, from three to four (1.2 to 1.6 in.).

### 9.—THE RIB.

This is flat, and placed on the last false ribs, near the flank. Its thickness for the first and second qualities is two centimetres (0.8 in.) and one centimetre (0.4 in.), on the third it is scarcely perceptible.

### 10.—THE FLANK.

This, called "the crust" by butchers, forms a layer of fat between the skin and flesh, and is characterized by small, soft, flat pellets of fat, rather long than round. It can be perceived by the undulating surface of the skin above it, and denotes the general state of plumpness. Its thickness is, for the respective qualities, two to three centimetres (0.8 to 1.2 in.), one and a half (0.6 in.), and one-half (0.2 in.).

### 11.—THE LOIN.

This manet, between the loins and the sides, presents a firm surface, called "the fat pavement" by butchers. On pinching between the tips of the fingers, it presents a thickness of two centimetres (0.8 in.) for the first quality.

### 12.—THE HAUNCH.

This is firm to the touch, and is found on the projecting part of the haunch, between the skin and the bone. For the first quality it shows a thickness of two and a half centimetres (1 in.).

### 13.—THE NECK-VEIN.

This lies along the jugular vein, and presents a sort of loose cord, which easily rolls under the fingers. For the first quality it has a thickness of from four to five centimetres (1.6 to 2 in.), for the second, from two to three (0.8 to 1.2 in.), and for the third, from one to two (0.4 to 0.8 in.). It denotes internal fat.

### 14.—THE EARLET.

This is short and of oval form, lying between the ear and the horn. It rolls loosely about under the skin, and may be compressed between the thumb and finger. For the first quality, it shows five to six centimetres (2 to 2.4 in.) thickness, two to three (0.8 to 1.2 in.) for the second, and one (0.4 in.) for the third.

### 15.—THE UNDER-JAW.

This is rather long than round, and lies in the bifurcation of the lower jaw. It may be felt crosswise with the fingers. Its thickness for the first quality is four to five centimetres (1.6 to 2 in.), three (1.2 in.) for the second, and one (0.4 in.) for the third.

## GENERAL REMARKS.

The size of the manets is proportioned to the fatness of the animal. Those which are firmest to the touch, indicate the finest quality of meat and greatest abundance of suet.

Whatever may be the size, the age, and the weight, cows and beeves of the first quality will give about fourteen to sixteen kilogrammes of tallow to the hundred kilogrammes of clear meat, the second quality from eight to ten, and the third from three to four. In this estimate I refer to the fat of the belly and intestines, not including the kidney-fat, which always goes with the hindquarters.

Bulls, as a rule, furnish a coarse and leathery meat, and have but little internal fat. The meat of fat heifers of from two to three years and a half, is usually of excellent quality; while at this age that of male animals is much inferior. The male does not attain his full development and perfect qualities until from six to eleven years. But it is not only sufficient that an animal should be fat, its fat and suet should be white, to make it of the first quality.

Those animals will give white fat which have the epidermis of the whole body white, or *café-au-lait* color; while those that show a yellow or pale orange epidermis will yield yellow fat. These colors sometimes depend upon the feeding; but in most cases they arise from the nature of the animal itself.

# CHAPTER IV.

## DOCILITY OF DISPOSITION.

By persistent and intelligent action, man has succeeded in domesticating various animals, among which the bovine species stands in the first rank, of which he has made a most valuable coadjutor in his toilsome labors, and a precious source of supply of his daily food. Buffon said, long ago: "Without the bovine species, both poor and rich would find it difficult to live : without it the land would lie untilled, upon it fall the hardest labors of agriculture. It is the most useful laborer on the farm, the main support of the rustic household, the principal force in agriculture, and the chief resource of a nation."

But cow and bull can not serve man perfectly, nor fulfill all his expectations, unless in addition to the three other qualities which I have dwelt upon, they possess a fourth : docility of disposition.

Like other creatures, these animals are born not only with good qualities, but also with defects, which, happily in most cases, can be overcome. Their education must begin at an early age; good and careful treatment will improve their disposition, but will not always entirely reform it. To attain this object great firmness and great gentleness are both necessary. Ill treatment generally results in rendering the animals ill-tempered, wild, or fierce. Some animals which have been subdued by a firm will, will only submit to the master who has conquered them, while in any other hands they are insubordinate and wild. Their natural disposition has been restrained, but not changed, and under altered conditions it shows in full force.

The male is naturally more intractable than the female, and at the rutting-time he often becomes unmanageable, and even fierce, and this disposition increases with age.

(125)

To subdue him, man has recourse to one of the modes of emasculation (*castration ou bistournage*), after which the animal becomes tractable, obedient, and fit for work.

———

# CHAPTER V.

## MEANS OF RECOGNIZING THE AGE OF CATTLE.

SUMMARY.—The Teeth.—The Horns.

### THE TEETH.

All the animals of this species are born with incisors, called "milk-teeth," which fall and are renewed at the periods which I shall mention. Calves born toothless are premature.

Bovine animals have thirty-two teeth, of which twenty-four are grinding-teeth, or molars, and eight are cutting-teeth, or incisors.

The molars serve for grinding the food in eating and in rumination; they are regularly distributed in four groups of six each, solidly planted. Two of these groups of molars form the entire dentition of the upper jaw, in which there are no incisors, but their place is filled by a mass of elastic cartilage forming a firm pad. The two other groups occupy the back of the lower jaw, and are separated by a space of about four inches, in which are planted the incisors.

The eight incisors in the front part of the lower jaw complete the dentition. They are grouped in a semi-circle, the middle ones being somewhat higher than those at the extremities. They are usually rather loose in the jaw, having but a single root.

At from two to two and a half years, the central incisors are lost, and replaced by the permanent teeth. From this time to three years, the two adjoining teeth are lost; six months later, the third incisors of each side; and at about four years the corner ones, all being replaced as they fall by the permanent teeth. It happens sometimes, but rarely, that the corner incisors are not lost.

When the permanent incisors have all appeared, the animal is rising five years. The molars of both jaws have been lost at about the same time, the four corresponding ones falling together, and being replaced by new ones. During this second dentition, and especially when cutting the permanent molars, the animal suffers more or less and eats with difficulty. It is well, if the suffering seems severe, or continues long, to have the loose tooth extracted by a skillful hand.

At five years, the teeth are usually complete and regular, the incisors forming a semicircle, of which the corner teeth are lower than those of the center. The upper surface of the tooth presents a sharp, projecting ring of enamel. After seven or eight years this symmetry is altered, the central incisors wearing down to about the height of the corners. After nine years, the enamel ring is worn down, the angles of the teeth show attrition, and the forms grow rounder. At from ten to twelve years, spaces begin to show between the teeth. At from fourteen to seventeen they are worn down to the roots, leaving wide interstices; the alveolar processes begin to be absorbed, and the teeth grow loose.

The rapidity of these changes depends to some degree upon the mode of life and the food of the animal. In heaths and sandy land the teeth wear out much faster, and animals raised in them may have the teeth quite worn away before they are old. In fertile pasturages, the teeth are preserved longer; but the dryness and perishing of the ivory occur at the ages above mentioned. When the incisors begin to fall, the animals have difficulty in grazing, and if intended for fattening, must be fed in the stall. Similar inconveniences follow the loss of one or more molars : the animal grinds its food with difficulty, and the jaw becomes more or less deformed.

Animals of this species are also subject to "wolf-teeth," which term is applied to teeth (usually the second molars) which grow long and pointed, interfering with the closure of the jaws and hindering mastication. Animals thus affected feed with difficulty, and are apt to pine away. The position of these teeth makes it difficult to inspect them ; but when discovered, the tooth should be cut or snapped off to the level of the rest.

The tongue also plays its part in feeding, gathering in the herbage to the mouth, where the incisors cut it off by pressure of their edges against the pad.

### THE HORNS.

In animals which have reached the age of three years, the horn has a ridge or ring at the base, and a new one is formed every year below the old one. But the number of these rings can not be relied upon in estimating the age, as it sometimes happens that in an old animal these rings are so blended that they can not be counted. In youth the horns are thickest at the base, and taper to a point; but when the animal has reached eight or ten years, a narrowing often takes place at the base, obliterating several rings. This is often the case with animals used for labor, as the pressure of the yoke and the friction of the parts which attach it to the horns, wear away the rings. The appearance of the horns is therefore a much more uncertain guide than that of the teeth, in estimating age; still, it should not be entirely neglected.

# CHAPTER VI.

## THE FEET.

The form of the feet is an indication of the nature of the place in which the animal has been reared. In stony regions the hoof grows round, and wears away; on the contrary in soft, moist, and marshy districts, the hoofs lengthen and flatten out, and the same effect is produced by confinement to the stable. The round hoof is a very desirable quality.

The false hoofs, commonly called "spurs" (*onglons*), when short, indicate that the young animal has a tendency to grow very large. If they are long or deformed, it shows that the animal has been raised in the stable, and will not readily accommodate itself to work or an open-air life.

Continued stall-feeding renders the feet so tender that after some years the animal can take no exercise, nor even comfortably wander over the pasture. The foot grows long and thick, and the creature is entirely unfitted for work or for driving to any distance.

# CHAPTER VII.

## ON THE CHOICE OF COWS.

The intending purchaser of a cow must be on his guard against a great variety of frauds and deceptions. When he has found an animal whose size, general figure, and color suit him, he should then examine the escutcheon, see to what class she belongs, and if she possesses the marks distinguishing the higher orders of the class. Care

(129)

must be taken not to be deceived by a false escutcheon, as dealers sometimes shave the hair from a part of the thighs and udder, so as to give an escutcheon of a low order the appearance of a higher. The yellowish or nankeen color is often imitated by staining the skin.

If the cow is with calf, the buyer should see if she still gives milk, and satisfy himself of the length of time she has been pregnant. If she be fresh, he must satisfy himself of the time elapsed since calving, if the delivery was satisfactory, and if there has been no inversion of the womb.

These examinations made, he can bargain for the price, and when a sum has been named which he is willing to give, he has a right to proceed to a more minute examination. He should make the cow walk before him, to see that her gait is easy and free. He should examine the muzzle, to see if it is moist and dewy, which is a sign of good health. He should open the mouth, to verify the age by the teeth, and to see that there are no aphthæ or ulcerations at the base of the tongue. He should notice if the breath is fresh and pure. Examine the eyes, to see if no humors are running from them, if there are no specks on the cornea, if the vessels are not blood-shot, if the pupil contracts, and the eyelids close readily.

He should examine the horns, to see if they are solid and have not been stained or operated on to conceal the marks of age. In the case of an animal intended for work, he should see that there are no wounds nor bruises on the nape of the neck or between the horns. He should also examine the forelegs, to make sure that there are no tumors, soft or hard, upon them, that the false hoofs are sound, and that there is no exudation in the space between them, nor in the folds of the pastern.

He will see if the hair is soft, the skin flexible and loose from the muscles. He will trace down all the ribs and false ribs, to see if there be any sign of wounds or of costal or umbilical hernias. Coming to the hind-quarters, he will examine if the udder be elastic and fleshy. If the teats are well shaped, not too near, and separated by regular intervals. If the "fountains" (cavities at the termination of the milk-veins) and the milk-veins are long, well-marked, and the latter tortuous. He will examine the vulva for ulcerations, and the hindlegs, as before he examined the forelegs.

I advise persons desirous of buying a milch cow to choose one nearly ready to calve, rather than one that is milking, as in the latter case there are more opportunities for deception. The udder of milch-cows offered for sale often appears of great size, when this is merely the result of leaving the cows unmilked for twenty-four hours; thus not only deceiving the buyer, but often injuring the animal, or diminishing its regular yield of milk, which is not recovered until a new calving, and sometimes not even then, if inflammation of the udder has resulted from this cruel trick.

If the system of examination which I have recommended be carefully carried out, the buyer can hardly be deceived very grossly, and will in all probability, even without previous experience, be able to select a good cow.

# The American Agriculturist

FOR THE

## Farm, Garden, and Household.

**Established in 1842.**

## The Best and Cheapest Agricultural Journal in the World.

TERMS, which include postage *pre-paid* by the Publishers: $1.50 per annum, in advance ; 3 copies for $4 ; 4 copies for $5 ; 5 copies for $6 ; 6 copies for $7 ; 7 copies for $8 ; 10 or more copies, only $1 each. Single Numbers, 15 cents.

# AMERIKANISCHER AGRICULTURIST.

The only purely Agricultural German paper in the United States, and the best in the world. It contains all of the principal matter of the English Edition, together with special departments for German cultivators, prepared by writers trained for the work. Terms same as for the "American Agriculturist."

# BOOKS FOR FARMERS AND OTHERS.

Send ten cents for our new handsomely illustrated and descriptive Catalogue of Books on all branches of Agriculture, Horticulture, Architecture, etc. All books comprised in this Catalogue will be mailed pre-paid on receipt of the price named. Our abridged descriptive Catalogue of Books will be sent free on application.

## Books on Out-Door Sports and Pastimes.

Send five cents for our new and elegantly gotten up SPORTSMAN'S COMPANION, containing brief descriptions or outlines of nearly one hundred and eighty works upon legitimate Out-door Sports and Amusements, and illustrated with a great number of engravings, many of them drawn from life, and faithfully portraying the points and characteristics of game, birds, fishes, horses, dogs, etc., etc.

**ORANGE JUDD COMPANY, 751 Broadway, New York.**

www.ingramcontent.com/pod-product-compliance
Lightning Source LLC
Chambersburg PA
CBHW032009010726
47493CB00007B/2334